GLORY! GLORY!

PIECES OF GOD'S STORY

GENESIS TO REVELATION IN RHYME

SHIRLEY VAUGHN-HAMMOND

Illustrated by Brenda Matthews

To: Delores Hayes
Shirley Vaughn

xulon PRESS

In loving memory of my husband, *DeHaven*

To **Pastor Cedric Brown**
who helped me recognize the
spiritual blank pages in my life
and whose own life and godly
teachings led me to expose
those empty spaces, nurture
them and kindle my relation-
ship with Christ.

Shepherd the flock of God among you...and not for sordid gain, but with eagerness; not yet as lording it over those allotted to your charge, but proving to be examples to the flock.
1 Peter 5:2, 3

To *you*—whomever or
wherever you happen to be—
who are lost and in need of the
Savior or who already know
Him but you know you truly
need to strengthen your walk
with Him through a conscience
commitment to daily reading
of the Word.

Your word is a lamp to my feet and a light to my path.
Psalm 119:105

CONTENTS

ACKNOWLEDGMENTS..xiii

PURPOSE...xv

POEMS TO HONOR THE OLD TESTAMENT 17

Genesis 19

Exodus 27

Leviticus 31

Numbers 35

Deuteronomy 39

Joshua 43

Judges 47

Ruth 51

1 Samuel 55

2 Samuel 61

1 Kings...67

2 Kings...73

1 Chronicles...77

2 Chronicles...81

Ezra...85

Nehemiah...89

Esther 93

Job 97
Psalms 101
Proverbs 105
Ecclesiastes 109
Song of Solomon 113
Isaiah 117
Jeremiah 121
Lamentations 127
Ezekiel 131
Daniel 137
Hosea 143
Joel 147
Amos 151
Obadiah 155
Jonah 157
Micah 161
Nahum 165
Habakkuk 169
Zephaniah 173
Haggai 177
Zechariah 181
Malachi 187

POEMS TO HONOR THE NEW TESTAMENT 191
Matthew 193
Mark 203
Luke 211
John 219
Acts 229
Romans 239
1 Corinthians 243
2 Corinthians 247
Galatians 253

Ephesians 257
Philippians 263
Colossians 269
1 Thessalonians 275
2 Thessalonians 279
1 Timothy 283
2 Timothy 289
Titus 293
Philemon 297
Hebrews 301
James 309
1 Peter...315
2 Peter...321
1 John..325
2 John..331
3 John..333
Jude...337
Revelation 341

ACKNOWLEDGMENTS

I praise God for choosing me and giving me the vision for this project, for His guidance in creating this book, and for the privilege of sharing it with you.

Words are inadequate to express thanksgiving to a special person who persevered through surgeries, pain and rehab and who—through it all—is still unrelenting. Thank you, Brenda, for your endurance and for your illustrations with expressive shadows of God's Word.

I am delighted to pile heaps of love upon my sister and brother, Marjorie Wade and William Vaughn, just for being my family. To everyone else who has ever touched my life, helped to shape it, and guided me toward learning and living God's Word, I am thankful.

Thank God for your heart, Lisa Brown, and for always being there for me whenever a need arises.

Thank you, Debbie Flores, for your steadfast thoughtfulness in calling me to make sure I'm okay—"alive and kicking"—and for all the times you took me away from my work just at the right moment which refreshed me and helped to keep me balanced. Thank you for those "seeking Him" questions. Never stop seeking Him!

Linda Vaughn—though miles away— you faithfully followed the progress of this book and nourished my soul with your friendship, your love and support. Glory be to God for placing you in my family!

I am so grateful to Spring Upshaw for allowing God to use her to help teach me invaluable insights. I am truly blessed to have her in my life.

Finally, I render tender thanks to my Christian family at **Commitment Community Church (striving to be God's best)** in Lindenwold, New Jersey who listened to my poems and blessed me with prayers and words of encouragement. I think of "home" when I think of you. *Love you!*

I thank my God…because of your partnership in the gospel.
Philippians 1:3, 5

PURPOSE

WHAT THIS BOOK IS NOT: This book is not a replacement for the Bible. These poems could never ever do justice to God's Word and they are not meant to do so.

This is merely a book of poems based on God's Word—one for each of the 66 books of the Bible. I sought to create these poems in wordage free and easy for most. Each poem attempts to lead you to the real thing—to God and His Word, the Bible, hoping that after you open up His pages and feast at His table, you will never hunger again!

Each poem offers a godly plea in the final verse or verses which beseeches the reader to seek to know the Word of God and to live the Word of God or, in case of the lost, to point them toward Christ and, ultimately, to lead them to salvation. After reading a poem, it is my prayer that you will be inspired and filled to the brim with an irrepressible urgency to reach for your Bible, to delve right into its life-giving hope and experience the power of the Lord. Then may you become committed to reading God's Word as a daily guide for your life here on earth as preparation for eternity.

Whether this book serves as a personal tool, as part of your church worship service or for special Christian events—retreats, seminars, luncheons, etc.—never stop there. Be consumed with curiosity and don't forget to follow up the poetry reading with the Holy Bible.

POEMS TO HONOR

THE OLD TESTAMENT

GENESIS

In the beginning God created the heavens and the earth.
1:1

God created man in His own image,
in the image of God He created him;
male and female He created them.
1:27

"And I will make you a great nation,
and I will bless you,
and make your name great;
and so you shall be a blessing…
And in you all the families of the earth will be blessed."
12:2-3

GENESIS

Oh, God! God of majesty, power, and purpose abounding
Because of Him and Him alone, all of life began
Suddenly He created the world so splendid and so new
As a significant part of His glorious and divine plan

God crowned His creation with male and female
In His own image He masterfully created the pair
Then they became one flesh in holy union
With the Garden of Eden provided for them to share

The Garden of Eden was Adam's designated charge
The tree of knowledge of good and evil was taboo
But when Eve was tempted by Satan and Adam consented
They chose to disobey God, causing sin to ensue

Sin swaggered right in and staked its claim on man
As Satan spread out his wares and became a wrecking-ball
The innocence of all creation was sorely shattered
The world was doomed and took an irreversible fall

Fellowship with God was severely splintered and frayed
As evil raised its tainted, pernicious, and deceptive head
Adam and Eve were banished forever from the Garden
And then Cain murdered Abel as iniquity continued to spread

Earth was no longer the paradise God had intended
As the human race exploded, expanded, and grew
God allowed humanity to change its sinful ways
But only Noah and his family were faithful and true

Seeing the great corruption of man on earth
Caused God's heart to break with grief and pain
So except for Noah who praised and obeyed Him
God destroyed the earth with a great flood of rain

Thereafter, God reassured Noah with a solemn promise
Never again shall the earth be destroyed by nature's tear
The rainbow shall be a sign of God's faithfulness to His Word
And the seasons shall come and go year after year

Then generations of Noah's sons replenished the earth
To make his descendants a great nation is what God planned
Most people ignored God and continued in their sin
But Abram obeyed and traveled to Canaan land

The Lord called Abram in the idolatrous city of Ur of the
Chaldeans
To embark on a life of pilgrimage from there to Canaan on
faith alone
God promised him Canaan, a great nation, prosperity, and
much more
His seed would be a channel of blessings to all, God's
heralding trombone

God set forth the holy vision of His plan for Abram's service
Decreeing His covenant people would be called His own
Abram, He commanded, must uphold faith and obedience
And the Savior would come through this chosen nation alone

With his wife Sarai and nephew Lot, Abram set out for an
unknown land
When famine struck, he chose to go to Egypt in order to survive
While there Pharaoh desired Sarai to be part of his harem
And Abram asked her to tell a lie in order to keep him alive

Before journeying to Egypt, Abram built an altar to the
Lord in Shechem and Ai
And to quell a dispute, he offered Lot his choice of
pastureland in true unselfishness
Lot chose the valley of the Jordan River and moved to the
sin-city of Sodom
Where he steadily delved into iniquity and indiscretion
which God couldn't bless

Though Abram yielded the land, his covenant with God
was his urgent mission
And after settling in the town of Hebron, he erected his
third altar to the Lord there
Then when he heard that his nephew Lot had been captured
by four invading kings
Abram and his men pursued the assailants and rescued him
by the sword and prayer

Later, not waiting on God, Sarai persuaded Abram to
impregnate Hagar, her maid
But when Hagar became pregnant, Sarai scorned her—
causing her to run away
Then as she set out for Egypt, an angel advised her to
return and submit to Sarai
And Abram was eighty-six when Ishmael was born to
Hagar on that particular day

Then God renewed His covenant, changing Abram's name
to Abraham, Sarai to Sarah
Agreeing Abraham would obey God's Word and circumcise
males in his family line

So God would give Abraham heirs, power, wealth, and
blessings beyond compare
Showing that His blessings outweigh what we give up
when we follow His holy design

Abraham was well along in years and despairing of ever
producing an heir
And Sarah, advanced in years too, was way pass the age to
bear a child
Yet God promised him descendants too numerous to count
or imagine
Still Sarah had doubts about God's vow and thought it was
quite futile

Sodom and Gomorrah were destroyed because of sexual
perversion, because of sin
Beforehand, two angels spared Lot and his family, escorting them
out of harm's way
In spite of being warned not to look behind or they would surely be
disposed of
Lot's wife looked back yearningly and became a pillar of salt on
that dreadful day

Sarah was ninety and Abraham one hundred when Isaac was born
Proving to them that everything is possible in God's mighty hand
And later when God asked Abraham to offer up Isaac as sacrifice
Abraham passed the test when he obeyed God's heart-rending
command

Isaac did not resist when he was about to be sacrificed by his father
And he gladly accepted Rebekah, chosen by a servant, as his bride
After the death of his father, Isaac inherited God's promise
to Abraham
To fulfill God's plan of making his descendants a great
nation as specified

Isaac and Rebekah were blessed with twin sons, Jacob and
Esau
Tragically, each twin was the definitive favorite of one
parent or the other
Eventually, Jacob duped Esau for his birthright with the
pleasure of food
Wrestled an angel, worked years to wed, and deceived his
father and brother

One of Jacob's sons, Joseph, was undoubtedly his father's
favorite
Clearly expressed in the coat of many colors he made for
Joseph alone
And Joseph's boastful attitude about dreams he related to
his brothers
Aggravated them, causing strained relationships to be
plainly shown

The hatred for Joseph festered inside his ten older brothers
And in time the jealousy grew, corroding into an ugly rage of dread
Then one day they conspired to get rid of him once and for all
So they sold him to slave traders, but told their father Joseph was
dead

Joseph was betrayed by his brothers and exposed to sexual
temptation
Punished for doing the right thing, imprisoned for quite a long time
And forgotten by those he had graciously helped along the way
Yet endured each setback because God boosted his upward climb

God's promises and faithfulness are manifest through Abraham
And by stories like those of Isaac, Jacob and Joseph—the three
In Genesis we clearly see how God uses all kinds of people
To bring hope and rebirth to everyone, even to you and me

Let a new day set the stage for discovering God's love
And stir revelations of truth and promise deep within
He longs to use you in this world of dwindling morality
To assure you of salvation, to save you from sin

In the beginning there was God
That's where Genesis begins
In the beginning there was God
Our Creator, Sustainer, and friend

Read Genesis and find God's purpose and plan for His creation
Read Genesis and be secure in God's promise of salvation
Read Genesis and feel the pulse of hope!

EXODUS

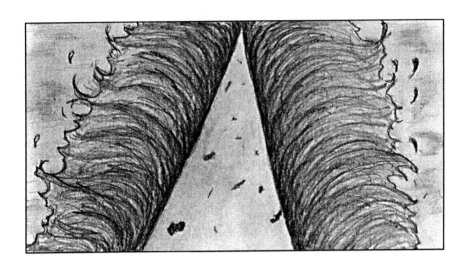

The LORD said, "I have surely seen the affliction
of My people
who are in Egypt, and have given heed to their cry
because of their taskmasters,
for I am aware of their sufferings."
3:7

"Therefore, come now, and I will send you to Pharaoh,
so that you may bring My people,
the sons of Israel,
out of Egypt."
3:10

EXODUS

Since Joseph moved his family to Egypt, four hundred
years had gone by
And the descendants of Abraham in great numbers did
indeed multiply
Egypt's new Pharaoh feared they'd threaten and upset his
kingdom though
Thus, he made them all slaves with oppression galore that
refused to let go

Then a boy named Moses became a prince in Pharaoh's
regal domicile
After his mother cautiously hid him as a baby by the banks
of the Nile
Which was all a part of God's plan to come to His people's
rescue
To liberate the Israelites, their lingering bondage eventually
to undo

After Moses grew up, one day slaves in hard labor were
dutifully engaged
Right there before his eyes—an Egyptian flogging a man—
he witnessed an outrage
When he thought no one was looking, Moses struck down
that perpetrator

So to escape punishment, he fled to Midian to be groomed
as Israel's liberator

As an outcast in the wilderness, Moses became a shepherd
in isolation
And God began preparing him to free Israel from Pharaoh's
domination
After speaking with God about his mission—with a burning
bush his agency
Moses agreed to return to Egypt to lead God's people out of
captivity

Pharaoh was confronted by Moses and Aaron as God
clearly had directed
And through a wave of plagues and promises made,
suspended or neglected
At last God delivered Israel from Pharaoh's cruel and
callous hand
Out of Egypt, through the Red Sea and onward, Moses led
by God's command

So that they'd know He was with them as they journeyed
day and night
God provided a pillar of cloud and fire for that mass of
humanity in flight
And though God showed His love and power, as toward
Canaan they did flee
They began to complain and yearn for their days back in
Egypt's captivity

God provided for their physical and spiritual needs as they
moved toward their goal
With food to partake and a place to worship, to nourish the
body and soul
But He also judged their disobedience as their
unfaithfulness did accrue
And sent forth the Ten Commandments and other standards
for living, too

Due to their great impatience at Moses' delay in coming
down from Mount Sinai
The people asked Aaron to make an idol for them and
Aaron proceeded to comply
He converted their gold earrings into a golden calf and all
worshiped it gleefully
And then Moses descended the mountain clutching two
tablets of the Testimony

He saw the people carrying on, in their lewd idolatrous and
wicked celebration
And in righteous anger, he broke the tablets as a witness of
their sinful adoration
Moses ground up the golden calf and Aaron implied it had
appeared mysteriously
And only because of Moses' intercession did the LORD
spare Aaron from fatality

If you are trapped or enslaved in some intolerable condition
you abhor
Or resist sacrificing the comfort and security you
wholeheartedly adore
Just listen to God for He's calling you to explore horizons
beyond the sun
Have faith and obey, and He will lead the way, for He's the
only one

Let Exodus excite you to God's Word and to His heavenly
connection
Give Him your heart and resolve to heed His moral and
holy directions

LEVITICUS

"You shall be holy,
for I the LORD your God am holy."
19:2b

LEVITICUS

The holiness of God and the sin that absolutely had to be
chastened
Called for the nation to listen attentively at the foot of
Mount Sinai
Thus through priests, animal sacrifices, and the sacred day
of atonement
The way was opened for the Israelites to worship God, only
Him to glorify

The Levites enlightened the people on how to worship with
their lives
They were the pastors, administrators, and such of their day
They managed moral, civil, and ceremonial laws as well
And took charge of the health, justice, and welfare in every
way

God provided directions for worship which would bring
Him pleasure
Which taught about His nature, about how to delight Him,
and to declare
That through perfect sacrificial offerings, obedience, and
symbols of repentance
The people had to see the gravity of sin and humble
themselves in prayer

Rules concerning cleanness and uncleanness were set forth
for all to obey
And anyone breaking a rule was forbidden to participate in
worship invariably
Those who became defiled were unfit for ritual until they
were made clean
Because in God's sight, holy people must be holy in all
areas, no fleshly liberty

God gave Israel implicit laws for living, for living a
spiritual holy life
Which should be separate and distinct from every pagan
nation
And believers must be alienated from sin and really
dedicated to God
To express praise, thanksgiving, and devotion in true
adoration

In order to give thanks and rededicate their lives to serving
only Him
There were feasts of celebration to remember what God
had done
In families and in fellowship and in quiet heartfelt
exaltation
To renew God's goodness in their lives—brothers and
sisters everyone

Moral and spiritual principles for health and sexual
conduct, too
Fleshly worldliness, relationships and family responsibility
Were set forth for daily living to make serving God well-
defined
And every rule linked with one's walk with God was a
sacred key

There were blessings for obedience to God, such as peace
and fruitfulness
As He does today, to lead His people to repentance, God
used adversity
Curses for disobedience to God were laid out so all would
be aware
Such as terror, disease, pestilence, invasion, and conquest
by the enemy

To show gratitude to the LORD, a man would make a vow
of his faithfulness
Such as a person, an animal, a house or a field—given in
consecration
And a tithe of land was required which to the LORD was
truly divine
Which helped the people grow in obedience for His honor
and glorification

We were created to have a close relationship with our
LORD
And when fellowship is broken, we are no longer content
and free
Let Leviticus lead you to be restored to God's pleasures and
desires
By praising and worshiping Him in faith and obedience
untiringly

Read Leviticus and see the holiness of God ingrained in
everything
The unholy cannot draw near to Him with their ungodly
deeds called sin
Read Leviticus and deal openly with your waywardness
and defiance
Then see God's blessings flow like mighty rivers over and
over again

NUMBERS

"Surely all the men who have seen My glory and My sign
which I performed in Egypt and in the wilderness,
yet have put Me to the test these ten times
and have not listened to My voice,
shall by no means see the land which I swore to their
fathers,
nor shall any of those who spurned Me see it."
14:22-23

NUMBERS

The nation of Israel was camped down below at the foot of
Mount Sinai
Having received God's laws and ready for the promised
land, now to unify
To figure out the number of men fit for the army to go to
war and stand
The LORD told Moses and Aaron to take a census of all the
males on hand

The people, set apart for God, were prepared for their
inheritance decree
In the camp He issued His people the rules for a life-style
of purity
Clear directions for being a holy people were provided
there for all
And the second Passover was observed by those obedient to
God's call

As the Israelites embarked upon their journey toward the
promised land
Moses dispatched spies to scout out territory, its inhabitants
they did scan
The people complained mightily about their hardship and
their lack of meat
About being stuck in the wilderness and facing staggering
and grave defeat

They openly rebelled against Moses and Aaron to weaken
their morale degree
They blamed them for the death of Korah and others in
order to get sympathy
They failed to trust God's promises or to own their
problems without dispute
They became greedy for power, instead of obeying God as
the true absolute

Because of their disobedience, their complaining and
rebellion gone awry
God punished the Israelites for unfaithfulness and
thousands did surely die
God declared that generation wouldn't live to see Canaan—
no quip, trick or ploy
So they were doomed to wander in the wilderness, never to
realize the joy

Years of aimless wandering resulted in no description of
any edification
They learned nothing from being punished for their sin and
depravation
So when the Israelites couldn't accept responsibility for
their unholy belief
They blamed Moses for their circumstance, for their
suffering and grief

When the people complained at Kadesh that no water was
available anywhere
To bring forth water from the rock was what the LORD did
graciously declare
But because Moses disobeyed God's authority in the
presence of everyone
He was forbidden to enter the promised land; no reprieve
would ever come

By and by—barring a handful—the old generation died, the
new poised to proceed
Ready to enter the land God had promised Israel many
years ago indeed
Then the LORD commanded Moses and Eleazar to count
heads—not one do ignore
And this second census of the new generation would be
recorded forevermore

Numbers tells the tragic story of Israel's defiance and
spiritual disbelief
Which added an extra forty years to their trek to Canaan
with oceans of grief
It also testifies that complaining and compromise bring
suffering and delay
And what happens when we yearn for sinful desires of
"good ole yesterday"

God's Word in Numbers must not be disregarded or tabled
'til tomorrow
If we are to claim God's promised land, avoid Israel's
mistakes and sorrow

DEUTERONOMY

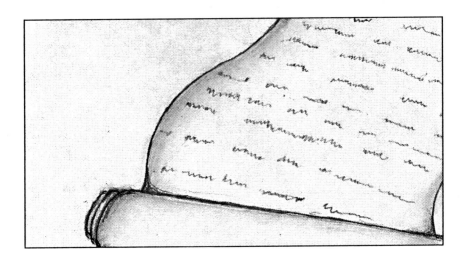

*"Know therefore that the LORD your God, He is God,
the faithful God, who keeps His covenant
and His lovingkindness to a thousandth generation
with those who love Him and keep His commandments."*
7:9

DEUTERONOMY

God had led Israel across the desert to Moab east of the
Jordan River
Now ready to enter the promised land, advice in review
Moses did deliver
To prepare the children of that bygone and unfaithful
generation crew
So they'd know God's laws, believe and obey Him in the
land they did pursue

Moses' first message recalled the history of God's care for
that fallen nation
So Israel would remember what God had done and to stress
His glorification
They were taught who they were—a people of sin, a people
apt to rebel
And were enlightened on grasping the way to relate to God
and others as well

Moses' second message recounted God's Ten
Commandments and other laws devised
He reminded them that obeying God brings blessings and
disobeying brings demise
And this disobedience holds consequences—not only in
this life, but into the next
For real life means commitment to God by faith, discipline
and a sacrificial context

Moses' third message reviewed the covenant God had made
with Israel forty years before
In which He promised to bless the Israelites as the chosen
nation he would underscore
And through whom the rest of the world would come to
know God, its only divine lifesaver
So Israel had to promise to obey God in order to receive
His holy approval and favor

Since the older generation broke its part of the covenant to
which they had agreed
Moses restated the agreement to the new with the results of
disobeying God's holy creed
To make them aware that disobedience comes from the
will, and ignorance doesn't apply
And know they should use God's Word, not limitations of
knowledge as a contrived alibi

After delivering the three sermons, Moses changed his style
of message into song
Which again gave a brief history of Israel and reminded
them of their blatant wrong
It warned them to avoid repeating those sins and offered
hope in trusting God's way
So if they ceaselessly turned away from sin, God would
save them without delay

God had given Moses power to grow from a stuttering
shepherd into a godly creation
Because of his courage, meekness and wisdom, he shaped
the slaves into a Hebrew nation
His love, respect, and faith in God was constant and strong
throughout his humble existence
He knew it wasn't greatness in him—but greatness in
God—that lifted him with persistence

Realizing his death was imminent, Moses delegated Joshua
to lead as was God's command
Though known as Israel's greatest prophet, Moses was not
allowed to enter the promised land
You see, he had disobeyed God years before when he took
credit for a miracle in Kadesh
But before he died, God let Moses climb atop Mount Nebo
to view Canaan—splendidly afresh

As you read Deuteronomy, may it remind you of all the
ways God loves you
May you learn from Israel's past so as not to repeat the
same mistakes, too
God's arms are outstretched, ready to catch us when we
stumble or fall
In Him we can always find refuge from our storms, with
faith the protocol

JOSHUA

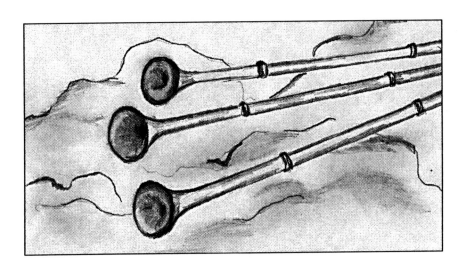

*"Pass through the midst of the camp and command
the people,
saying, 'Prepare provisions for yourselves,
for within three days you are to cross this Jordan,
to go in to possess the land
which the LORD your God is giving you,
to possess it.' "*
1:11

*"If it is disagreeable in your sight to serve the LORD,
choose for yourselves today whom you will serve. . . .
but as for me and my house, we will serve the LORD."*
24:15

JOSHUA

Although the older generation had failed God and wouldn't
enter the promised land
They taught the new generation to obey so they wouldn't
suffer, so they'd understand
As they wandered in the wilderness, they learned obedience
to God and furthermore
They reminded the new of the joy of doing God's will, of
the pain if they ignore

Now Joshua accepted the challenge and submitted to God
as he led that nation
Setting out across the Jordan to fulfill God's plan (once
Moses' obligation)
God parted the water to let them enter Canaan, crossing on
dry and wondrous ground
Then as God commanded, they built a memorial—a
reminder of a miracle so profound

Everyone agreed to obey Joshua as commander in order to
conquer the land
Then Joshua sent spies to scout out the area in pursuit of
securing the upper hand
Rahab, a prostitute, hid the spies on her rooftop and misled
the powers-that-be
Willing to risk all—with some sense of God, she and her
house received security

Canaan was a bastion that rebelled against God with its
practice of idolatry
The first city to fall was Jericho, proving idols are inferior
to God's invincibility
The Canaanites were a threat to God's way of living and
had to be annihilated
So that the Israelites' conduct would be righteously secured
and uncontaminated

After Joshua and his army conquered Jericho, they were
defeated at Ai due to sin
Because Achan looted their possessions following the battle
of Jericho and then
God held the whole nation responsible and banned the
covenant right away
The people knew such behavior wasn't tolerated, knew the
price they would pay

Achan and his family were stoned and burned; then Israel
was cleansed of her sin
So when Joshua attacked again, they burned the city—
realizing a crucial win
Subsequently, Joshua moved from city to city cleansing
Canaan of iniquity
From the south to the north, the land was steadily purged of
its wicked idolatry

Though much of the land was unconquered, after battling
for seven years straight
Israel gained control of the land and God's people were set
to receive their estate
Canaan was divided among the twelve tribes as God
Himself desired it should be
The promised land was Israel's inheritance, but even more,
an inheritance spiritually

Joshua, now advanced in years, called the people together
to refresh and to advise
To help them where they were apt to fall, since knowing
one's weakness is always wise
He counseled them to follow the laws, to cling to the
LORD without any deviation
And not to associate or intermarry with pagans, for such
only invites temptation

Later, Joshua called all the tribes of Israel to review their
unique and obligatory history
And challenged them to always choose to serve the LORD
all their days, even to eternity
Boldly they claimed they would never forsake God, but
would obey Him and Him alone
But do you think they really kept their promise after Joshua
was dead and gone?

Read the book of Joshua and observe his commitment to
obeying God exclusively
"But as for me and my house, we will serve the LORD,"
Joshua stressed as noteworthy
Decide today to follow the LORD—no matter where He
leads, no matter the price
Come together with others who believe in Him; come and
make the sacrifice

JUDGES

In those days there was no king in Israel;
every man did what was right in his own eyes.
17:6

JUDGES

Canaanites were worshipers of pagan gods, a nation full-
fraught with idolatry
And God charged Israel with destroying that wretched and
iniquitous society
Although Jerusalem and other cities were toppled, were
thoroughly defeated
After Joshua's death, the conquest of Canaan was really
never completed

So the LORD withdrew His promise to help Israel wipe out
her enemies
And would no longer protect her and bless her in the battle
vicinities
One generation died out and the next rebelled against
God—yes, they disobeyed
By resorting to idol worshiping, their faith in the LORD
wavered and decayed

Then came cycles of sinning, idolatry, judgment—begging
God's help from oppression
So God would send a judge to deliver the people from their
recurring transgressions
Now Israel would obey for awhile, but then fall back into
the worldly pits of idolatry
And the gruesome cycle would just start all over again,
from sin to delivery

For over three hundred years this sequence was repeated—
a sad, rhythmic routine
Covering six periods of bondage under the Mesopotamians
and to the Philistines
Twelve judges in all were used by God during those cycles
of repeated sin
Deborah, Gideon, and Samson are just three God used to
reel the sinners back in

Israel was the nation God chose to set the pace for living
holy, for living righteously
But her people were enthralled in moral decay, seated in
violence and idolatry
They followed their own selfish desires instead of obeying
God, His laws and directions
They relied on themselves and did what they pleased with
no kind of godly reflection

One lesson to be learned from Judges is as clear as clear
can be
When we repeatedly wallow in sin and refuse to learn from
history
When we live only for the moment, shun God and foolishly
depart
Consequences will surely ensue with suffering for the
sinful heart

Judges also teaches that when God gives us a mission to
fulfill
We shouldn't seek approval from society; it can kindle our
fleshly will
But above all, God shows us His mercy, no matter how
often we sin
No matter our missteps, our blunders, He'll deliver us again
and again

RUTH

But Ruth said, "Do not urge me to leave you
or turn back from following you;
for where you go, I will go,
and where you lodge, I will lodge.
Your people shall be my people,
and your God, my God."
1:16

RUTH

During the period of the judges, the story of Ruth takes
place
Those were dark and evil days of crisis, of despair and
disgrace
But even amidst such wicked times, there were those who
didn't stray
Who kept the LORD in their hearts and let Him use them
His way

In the time of the exodus from Egypt, the Moabites had
strongly resisted
And wouldn't let the Israelites pass through their land as
they had insisted
So the Moabites weren't allowed to worship at the
tabernacle—no way, not ever
And to marry a Canaanite was an unthinkable act for them
to even endeavor

But it happened one day in Moab that Naomi's dear
husband died
Her two sons married Oprah and Ruth and within ten years
also expired
Then Ruth gave up the likelihood of having children and
security
In order to care for Naomi, the Israelite, and save her from
beggary

Ruth belonged to a race that Israel had many times
disregarded and despised
But because of her faith she was blessed by God and by
Him was recognized
When Ruth's mother-in-law advised her to go back to her
own people to dwell
Ruth informed Naomi she'd follow her anywhere and
accept her God as well

So Naomi returned to Bethlehem with Ruth, the Moabite,
close by her side
And when Boaz heard she'd stood by Naomi after her
husband died
And how she had left her motherland behind to come to a
foreign nation
He let her glean grain in his field, showing her much
consideration

Since Naomi had no more sons, the law during that time
provided
That her closest relative was allowed to marry Ruth if he so
decided
When the closest relative backed down, Boaz purchased her
son's land
And took Ruth as his wife, after she'd followed Naomi's
plan

Out of Naomi's and Ruth's tragedies, God truly blessed
them without end
For throughout tough times and uncertainty, they trusted
Him again and again
Although Ruth was unaware of the bigger purpose for her
existence on earth
She became a part of God's design and lineage to the
Messiah's promised birth

Read the book of Ruth and know that God has a purpose
for your life today
Which will reach beyond your lifetime—by choices you
make, by how you obey
Your noblest blessing may not be acquiring money,
marriage or information
Try love and respect—and drawing family and others to an
invitation to salvation

Read Ruth and wipe away your tear
Read Ruth and let distress disappear

1 SAMUEL

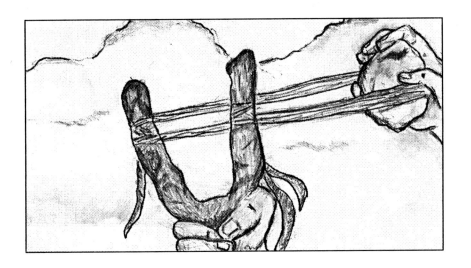

The LORD said to Samuel, "Listen to the voice
of the people
in regard to all that they say to you,
for they have not rejected you,
but they have rejected Me from being king over them...
and tell them of the procedure
of the king who will reign over them."
8:7, 9b

"For God sees not as man sees,
for man looks at the outward appearance,
but the LORD looks at the heart."
16:7b

1 SAMUEL

When judges ruled Israel, Samuel was the last judge in the wing
He was also her first priest and prophet during the time of a king
Samuel set the pace for all as to what a good judge should be
Because he was governed by God's Word, not by his own
policy

Now Hannah, who could not conceive and antagonized by
her adversary
Went year after year to the house of the LORD to pray
there customarily
She prayed and wept in great distress, then she promised
she'd allow
Her child dedicated—all the days of his life—to the LORD
as a solemn vow

In time Hannah was blessed with a son and named him
Samuel on that day
And when he was weaned, to the house of the LORD she
took him without delay
Then to thank Him for her child, Hannah worshiped God in
praise and in song
For she saw God as the all-knowing one—as unchanging,
firm and strong

As Eli's helper in the tabernacle, Samuel served with verve
and dignity
He served his holy God there as well, taking his job quite
seriously
Eli's own blood sons were evil, but he failed to read them
the riot act
And let his two sons treat God's offerings with contempt
and dishonor, in fact

Eli was guilty of honoring his sons above God with their
bold and sinful appetite
He also cared more about religious symbols than
representing God's holy light
God issued warnings to Eli and revealed the penalty if he
didn't heed and submit
So for neglecting his responsibilities, his sons would pay
the price their sins befit

Although Eli was older than Samuel and more experienced
in the priestly way
God called Samuel to be a prophet, all based on faith and
his will to obey
God spoke to Samuel and judged Eli's house forever for its
ongoing deviltry
His sons had brought a curse on themselves and Eli
rebuked not their atrocity

When war erupted between Israel and her enemy, those
warring Philistines
Israel was defeated when thousands expired on the brutal
battlefield scene
Eli's sons carried the ark of the covenant to Israel's
vanquished combat field
Some people thought it would protect them from the
power-of-the-war ordeal

But Israel was defeated once again and thirty thousand
Israelites died
The Philistines snatched the ark of God and Eli's wayward
sons expired
Then when Eli heard about the theft, he fell, broke his neck
and ceased to be
Then God afflicted the Philistines with awful tumors for
their act of thievery

After many maneuvers and circumstances, the ark of God
was finally returned
And sorrow gripped Israel for twenty years because she just
refused to learn
Then Samuel told his people if they'd turn back to God and
serve Him exclusively
After renouncing their idols, God would save them from
the Philistines in victory

Samuel judged Israel well all of his life and led the people
back into God's hand
And when he was old, he appointed his sons to replace him
as leaders of the land
But alas! His two sons were corrupt and wouldn't drink
from God's holy spring
So the elders of Israel decided that Samuel must appoint the
nation a worthy king

Saul was chosen by God, anointed by Samuel and picked
publicly as king of the nation
Samuel fervently charged him to answer only to the Lord
with righteous reputation
Though God disagreed with instituting a king, He let
Samuel select Saul to turn the tide
Then Saul defeated the Ammonites and his kingship was
validated, his rule verified

Samuel continued to pray for Israel and to teach
righteousness to everyone
In his farewell speech, he reminded them of the great things
God had done
He said they should serve the LORD faithfully, being
sincere and appreciative
That if they didn't cease their wickedness, they wouldn't be
allowed to live

But Saul disobeyed God, substituting ritual for faith in
God—displaying no loyalty
He became rebellious and arrogant, so God took away his
kingdom—a vital urgency
Saul ruled Israel forty-two years and still reigned when
Samuel named his replacement
God sought out a man after His own heart as ruler and
David was the one He sent

Young David conquered Goliath and Saul's son Jonathan
became his lifelong friend
When Saul realized David would be king, he set out to
bring his life to an end
The jealousy grew and repeatedly he tried to murder David,
but each time he failed
He used his daughter's marriage to David to plot his death,
to pursue David's trail

David spared Saul's life and promised never to take revenge
on his family or his heir
Then Samuel passed away and Israel had no spiritual leader
till David became king there
After her husband's death, David married Abigail and
spared Saul's life once again
Then Saul was defeated by the Philistines and, falling on
his sword, his life met its end

Read 1Samuel and learn that sacrifices are empty without
obedience and love
That religion is never sufficient—you must be devoted to
the LORD your God above
1 Samuel will show you that if you are irresponsible with
what God has charged you
Ultimately you'll use up your excuses, but still must give
account for whatever you do

Read 1 Samuel and see that appearances don't reveal what
you're really all about
That society may judge physical traits rather than good
character that's pure and devout
1 Samuel demonstrates how tough times in life help prepare
us for what God has in store
And no matter the suffering we might endure, God's in
control today and forevermore

2 SAMUEL

*And David realized that the LORD
had established him as king over Israel,
and that He had exalted his kingdom
for the sake of His people Israel.
5:12*

2 SAMUEL

After hiding from Saul for years, finally David heard that
Saul and Jonathan were dead
Rather than making merry, he mourned, played the harp
and chanted a lament instead
Then David asked God for counsel and God directed him to
Hebron in sanctity
Samuel had already anointed David king, so now Judah
anointed him publicly

To accept David as king, for seven-and-a-half years Israel
utterly did refuse
But finally he was crowned king over all of Israel—the one
God wanted to use
Afterward, he assumed the task of subduing his enemies, of
wrapping up God's plan
To complete the job Israel had failed to do when they
entered the promised land

He knew he must put that mule to rest in order for Israel to
explicitly unite
Which would protect the nation from her antagonists,
lurking constantly to fight
But before David went into battle, he petitioned the LORD
for guidance, for direction
Because he knew his strength and greatness came only
through God's connection

Though God said no to David's request to build the
LORD'S temple while he was king
God promised to continue his kingdom forever with heirs
which He would bring
Then David humbled himself and accepted God's promise
of extending his dynasty
For he realized that through Israel the whole world would
be blessed, blessed mightily

Deciding not to go into battle one spring day, David stayed
home from the battlefield
And from his roof, he saw Bathsheba bathing and his greed
and lust were revealed
He didn't flee temptation that evening, but committed
adultery straightaway instead
And later he had her husband killed—blinded by *sin
finding you out* just as God said

When the time of grieving was over, Bathsheba became
David's wife and then
David sorely regretted what he had done and asked God for
forgiveness of his sin
After Bathsheba bore him a son, God let the child die—the
price David must pay
But sometime later, she gave birth to Solomon who would
succeed his throne one day

It happened that David's son Ammon faked illness to
commit an incestuous and selfish act
With support from his cousin Jonadab, he raped his half-
sister Tamar—what a heinous attack!
Then he had her thrown out, making it appear that she had
made the sinful proposition
In time Absalom had Ammon killed for raping his sister—
his secret and personal mission

Afterward, Absalom conspired to steal the hearts of the
people, to be king by trickery
Which caused a national rebellion to arise, so off to
Jerusalem David was compelled to flee
Following many struggles and assorted tragedies, he was
restored as king of the nation
Finally, after four hundred years, Israel was at peace due to
David's godly dedication

Woven within David's reign was Nathan—a prophet, a
counselor, and a fearless friend
Who was always willing to advise David with truth, even if
it caused pain in the end
He confronted David's sins of betrayal and lying, of
murder, of theft and adultery
He reminded him of the cost sin generates, but was also
comforting and trustworthy

David was used by God to lead his people, but had
problems in family relations
He failed to realize that undisciplined children become
undisciplined adult sensations
And children cannot grow spiritually and morally or
fabricate faith upon request
Unless disciplined while young, with ample attention—
patient rearing being addressed

David's life teaches us that sin creates suffering which
doesn't rival fleeting pleasure
And temptation creeps in when your life lacks purpose,
when God isn't your treasure
Even a man after God's own heart can slip into the world,
into its dregs of sin
So don't excuse sin in your own life even if you've
prospered time and time again

Read 2 Samuel and see David's faithfulness, his
commitment—see his honesty
Grasp the lesson and learn from his sins, from his change of
heart, from his agony
Read 2 Samuel and realize that covering up your sin will
only multiply the pain
Grasp the lesson and know that God will always forgive,
strengthen and remain

1 KINGS

*"As for you, if you walk before Me
as your father David walked,
in integrity of heart and uprightness,
doing according to all I have commanded you
and will keep My statutes and My ordinances,
then I will establish the throne of your kingdom
over Israel forever, just as I promised to your
father David, saying, 'You shall not lack a man on the
throne of Israel.'"
9:4-5*

1 KINGS

King David was well advanced in age as his health was
skidding to its gravest degree
When his fourth son, Adonijah, decided to usurp the
throne—oh, so deceptively!
But his fallacious plan didn't work and he was caught in his
own slippery scheme
Straightaway, his brother Solomon was anointed king with
rich rejoicing in extreme

Now David charged Solomon to make God the center of his
life and his kingdom as well
To make sure his enemies received the punishment
deserved, even to the depths of hell
Then David died—having reigned over Israel forty years
which he righteously directed
Subsequently, Solomon executed his enemies, except for
just one man who was rejected

When God asked Solomon in a dream one night what he
wished the Lord to give
Solomon requested an understanding heart and wisdom in
order to lead and live
He did not ask for material things, for selfish services,
pleasures or for deeds
So God gave him both riches and honor, and a long life was
granted, was guaranteed

Because he sought God's direction, Solomon used his
wisdom well during his reign
And applying this wisdom brought peace, stability and
prosperity within Israel's domain
He also wrote thousands of proverbs and a multitude of
songs which are quite noteworthy
And he built the temple with great care, with honor and
respect for God's holy sanctuary

But against God's will, Solomon married many foreign
women and away from God was led
Though known as the wisest man who ever lived, they
swayed him to worship idols instead
Solomon continued to dabble in evil and eventually his
kingdom was corrupted by sin
No longer was he interested in God, so he lost everything as
his reign came to an end

Solomon's rule over Israel lasted forty years and then he
departed this earthly life
Thereafter, the kingdom divided into two nations and the
effect was disaster and strife
Each king and priest were unfaithful and wicked, and
encouraged people into idolatry
So for 300 years God called prophets to rescue Israel from
spiritual decay and immorality

You see, Judah in the south had housed two evil kings and a
couple of good ones, too
And vacillated between godly and ungodly living, wrapped
up in sin which grew and grew
Israel in the north, with eight evil kings in succession,
drifted right along in iniquity
So God punished both kingdoms for going their own way
and sent each one adversity

Elijah was the first of a stream of prophets God sent to the
nations to deliver His Word
Elijah confronted and challenged the people to take a stand,
to stand for God undeterred
For they had abused their privileges and God's Word had
been scorned and undermined
So Elijah's ministry carried the urgent task of calling that
nation back to God's design

Elijah predicted the beginning and the end of a drought and
restored a dead child back to life
Through prayer, he could bring down God's blessings like
rain and even bring wrath or strife
He anointed kings over Syria and Israel and a farmer,
Elisha, who'd succeed him eventually
Who left all to follow Elijah and become his servant until
time for transfer of authority

Through Elijah, God worked an amazing miracle when the
prophets of Baal were defeated
But Queen Jezebel retaliated by threatening his life, so
Elijah ran—feeling highly mistreated
Though God provided food and shelter in the wilderness,
he felt abandoned and wished to die
So God came to Elijah with visions and a gentle message,
necessary to open his mindless eye

Elijah wrestled with his feelings even after God's message
of comfort and enlightenment
But God challenged his emotions, called him to action,
revealing his next duty as imminent
He informed Elijah that part of his loneliness was due to
ignorance he hadn't perceived
And an extraordinary and personal life with God was what
he must realize and achieve

In spite of inconceivable opposition, Elijah is one of the
greatest prophets in Biblical history
Standing for God, he served the LORD in obedience—
proving one plus God is a majority
But Jezebel—who rejected God—is known as the most evil
woman the Bible ever scribed
Her determination to make Israel idol worshipers was one
cause of its fall, of its great demise

Read 1 Kings and discover that God—not humans who
ignore Him—is your only authority
That wrongdoing can gradually corrupt and turn into a way
of life for anyone invariably
Read 1 Kings and discover that if you sanction whatever is
desirable just for a song
Sooner or later you'll find you've been worshiping a false
god—*yourself*—all along

Read 1 Kings and discover that you are never alone, God is
always there
Seek Him in busy and quiet places, happy and sad places—
seek Him everywhere

2 KINGS

Yet the LORD warned Israel and Judah
through all His prophets and every seer, saying,
"Turn from your evil ways and keep My commandments,
My statutes according to all the law
which I commanded your fathers,
and which I sent to you through My servants the
prophets."
However, they did not listen,
but stiffened their neck like their fathers,
who did not believe in the LORD their God.
17:13-14

2 KINGS

God's prophet, Elijah, was carried away to heaven in a
whirlwind without dying
Then Elisha succeeded Elijah as Israel's chief prophet—
another hope for unifying
Through Elijah, God performed seven miracles and through
Elisha he worked ten
In order to help the needy and show His might and power
over pagan idols of men

Elisha served to restore respect for God and His Word
throughout Israel's domain
He took a stand against the evil kings and revealed God's
mercy for those who sustained
The evil kings encouraged pagan worship, using priests and
prophets to manipulate
They were shortsighted and by fostering other religions,
tried controlling their nation's fate

The good kings had to spend most of their time dismantling
the evil of their predecessors
In both Israel and Judah, Hezekiah and Josiah were the
only two good king successors
The Babylonian army seized Jerusalem, burned the temple
and took the people into captivity
Judah was exiled, but God kept His spiritual kingdom alive
in the hearts of many expellees

Read 2 Kings and learn that from this captivity, Israel and
Judah never really did return
A dark age for God's people occurred due to sin which
scarred and sorely burned
The end comes to those who shut God out of their lives and
reject His commands
Who don't let Him enter as Master, as counselor, to become
part of His perfect plan

Read 2 Kings and see the results of making things more
important than His glory
When we become anesthetized to the world and can't see
God's plan for our brief story
Like the people of Judah and Israel, we may falter, but God
promises never to bend
He's always there to guide us, to set our lives straight, and
help us start over again

1 CHRONICLES

And David knew that the LORD
had established him as king over Israel
and that his kingdom had been highly exalted,
for the sake of his people Israel.
14:2

Then he died in a ripe old age,
full of days, riches and honor;
and his son Solomon reigned in his place.
29:28

1 CHRONICLES

1 Chronicles begins with Adam and summarizes the
ancestry of Israel's history
It accentuates the Jewish heritage in trying to unite the
nation region-wise and spiritually
It was written after their captivity and stresses godly truths
designed to open their eyes
David's royal line and triumphs are underscored, but his
sins are by no means scrutinized

By reiterating Israel's history in its genealogies and stories
of the various kings
The spiritual foundation for the nation is recorded with the
promises God brings
The story of David's life and his relationship with God are
significant narrative accents
It depicts His devotion to God and His Word, to the people
and to justice unbent

God defined Israel's heritage from the family of Adam,
from generation to generation
Its nation in Abraham, its priesthood under Levi, its
kings—like David— for preservation
David's life shows us how important it is to study and obey
God's Word everyday
Get set for 2 Chronicles and observe how our lives worsen
when we're unwilling to obey

Read 1 Chronicles and observe that devoted service to God
must be our highest goal
How He is always faithful, always protects and provides
and must be our sole control
It prompts us to see the need for tracing our roots, for
unveiling our spiritual foundation
To continue to recommit to passing on a genuine and holy
faith to the next generation

2 CHRONICLES

*"If I shut up the heavens so that there is no rain,
or if I command the locust to devour the land,
or if I send pestilence among My people,
and My people who are called by My name
humble themselves and pray and seek My face
and turn from their wicked ways,
then I will hear from heaven,
will forgive their sin and will heal their land."*
7:13-14

2 CHRONICLES

In response to Solomon's prayer, God granted wisdom,
wisdom utterly unparalleled
And because he put God first, God gave him immense
wealth, riches and honor as well
Then Solomon built the temple God had previously allowed
David to plan and prepare
And at its first service of dedication, he knelt before God to
express reverence in prayer

Solomon married Pharaoh's daughter and other women
who worshiped idols devotedly
He knew these marriages weren't blessed by God, but was
contrary to God's holy decree
Although he diligently followed God's plan for building the
temple and offering sacrifice
It was written how he disobeyed, shadowing his pagan
brides—shunning God's advice

Although Israel prospered tremendously during the time
Solomon reigned as king
And testified to God's power and love and his faithfulness
embodied in everything
Ultimately, the good days faded as his pagan wives insisted
on generating sin
And sadly Solomon slipped far away from God, causing his
downfall in the end

After Solomon's death, his son Rehoboam reigned, but he
was foolish and unwise
Which divided the kingdom into two nations—with unity
far from being realized
With Judah's alternating years of rebellion and reform—
from obedience to abandonment
From one reign to another, a few good kings and many evil
ones were continually evident

2 Chronicles again repeats Israel's history, aiming to
reunite the nation after captivity
Especially to bring the people together in order to worship
God in truth and sanctity
But Judah's failure to repent resulted in God's judgment,
powerfully demonstrated
And the nation was eventually conquered, held captive, and
the temple desolated

Read 2 Chronicles and glean the lesson of hollow and
casual commitment to God our King
When we forget that all we are or hope to be comes from
Him and the promises He brings
Then we put ourselves at risk of facing Israel's same
spiritual and moral collapse today
Yet when our lives seem disheveled and hopeless, He
abides—waiting for us to obey

EZRA

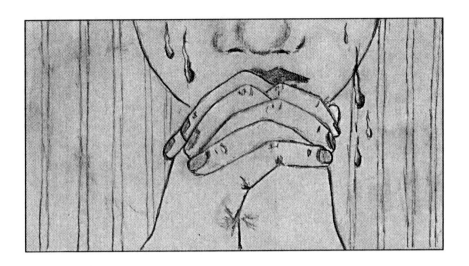

The sons of Israel who returned from exile
and all those who had separated themselves
from the impurities of the nations of the land
to join them
to seek the LORD God of Israel, ate the Passover.
6:21

"O my God, I am ashamed and embarrassed
to lift up my face to You, my God,
for our iniquities have risen above our heads
and our guilt has grown even to the heavens."
9:6

EZRA

Babylon was overthrown by Persia where Cyrus was king
after Nebuchadnezzar died
Then Cyrus allowed a group of exiled Jews to return to
their homeland, as was prophesied
The people rebuilt the temple in approximately four years
and then it was dedicated
And in order to commemorate Israel's deliverance from
Egypt, Passover was celebrated

Years later Ezra returned to Jerusalem with the second
group of Jewish exiles
He opposed the Israelites' marriage to pagan women which
caused sin, so dark and vile
After learning about these evil deeds, Ezra confessed the
sins of his people in prayer
And ordered the men to send their wives packing to save
Judah from spiritual despair

Subsequently, the people confessed their sins to God and
asked for His direction
So as to restore their relationship with the LORD, with
behavior and attitude correction
Whoever would choose not to meet within three days,
according to the leader's stand
Would be expelled from the assembly of the exiled and lose
the right to own any land

Read the book of Ezra and you'll discover that God can
rebuild, can truly restore
You're never so far away from Him that you can't catch
sight of that wide-open door
It doesn't matter how far you've strayed or how long
you've been away
God is able to repair your relationship with Him and
rebuild your life today

NEHEMIAH

So the wall was completed on the twenty-fifth
of Elul, in fifty-two days.
When all our enemies heard about this,
and all the surrounding nations were afraid
and lost their self-confidence,
because they realized that this work
had been done
with the help of our God.
6:15-16

NEHEMIAH

The homecoming exiled Jews had now been in Jerusalem
for many a year
But the walls of the city remained crumbled and disrepair
was quite clear
Which left the people unprotected and vulnerable to any
lurking enemy
So the Jews were in need of leadership to direct lives and
labor competently

Nehemiah, the king's cupbearer, heard that the wall had not
been rebuilt yet
And he was deeply grieved over the news, so he sat down,
mourned and wept
Afterwards, he fasted and prayed, searching for ways to
rectify the situation
And his prayer was answered when the king let him go to
his requested location

Nehemiah secured letters from the king to pass through
provinces along the way
And asked for timber for rebuilding the wall, which the
king granted without delay
Nehemiah arrived in Jerusalem and was greeted by some
leaders with opposition
But he kept his plans secret to keep rivals away from his
God-nurtured mission

When Nehemiah and citizens began rebuilding the wall,
they were ridiculed by some
Yet they did not lose faith, but persevered, and their
discouragement was overcome
When rich Jews used the plight of the returned exiles for
much profit and greed
Nehemiah confronted them face to face and usury was
swiftly abolished indeed

When the enemies were trying to frighten them and
discourage them from taking a stand
Nehemiah didn't ask God for release from the job, but
prayed He'd strengthen his hands
Then two officials plotted to halt construction of the wall
which was almost complete
Their plan was to ambush Nehemiah, but Shemaiah warned
him of their awful deceit

The wall was rebuilt in fifty-two days, but many lives
needed rebuilding spiritually
So Nehemiah gathered the people together and Ezra read
God's law as a remedy
As they realized their sins, they openly wept, and repented
to the Lord, too
They had to reaffirm their faith and ask God to become the
center of all they do

So once again the agreement God had made with Moses
and His people was restored
They agreed to be responsible and would not allow God
and His Word to be ignored
They vowed to follow Him and keep His laws with all their
hearts and do it seriously
And to keep their promise to God whether experiencing
hard times or prosperity

Read Nehemiah and notice that it's often necessary to wait
and just stand firm
Not only for leaders like Nehemiah, but a lesson all God's
people should learn
Read Nehemiah and notice that being a leader can appear
full of fascination
But can be thankless, lonely, pressure-filled-to-
compromise, without appreciation

Read Nehemiah and notice that there can be no success
without risk of defeat
And no reward without hard work, without criticism or
elements of deceit
But above all, there can be no true leader without God as
your shield and guide
For when you lose sight of Him, your life begins to topple,
your spirit is denied

Remember there's a place for everyone in God's plan,
whatever your status may be
He might use you in an unexpected way to fulfill His
purpose, might use you deliberately
So read Nehemiah and notice a remarkable testimony to
God—may its message be heard
Then resolve to be someone upon whom God can rely to
execute His heavenly Word

ESTHER

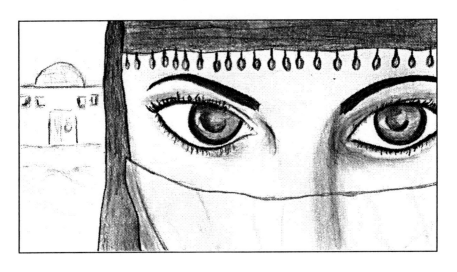

"For if you remain silent at this time, relief and
deliverance
will arise for the Jews from another place
and you and your father's house will perish.
And who knows whether you have not attained royalty
for such a time as this?"
4:14

ESTHER

When Queen Vashti refused to display her beauty before
the king's male company
And unwilling to obey her intoxicated husband, he
banished her accordingly
Then he sent out a decree to gather every beautiful young
virgin to be scrutinized
From all selectees, King Ahasuerus chose Esther and
making her queen was finalized

Mordecai had adopted Esther, his cousin, when her mother
and father passed away
Just as before, when she became queen, he still watched out
for her each and every day
Then one day, sitting at the king's gate, a plot to kill the
king was revealed to Mordecai
So Esther called for the Jews to fast and in turn informed
the king of the conspiracy cry

Subsequently, overly ambitious Haman was appointed
second-in-charge within the empire
All the servants at the king's gate were ordered to bow and
pay homage to him as he required
But Mordecai refused and Haman, who hated Jews, was
enraged and plotted to kill them all
Then in order to save her people, Esther risked her life after
learning about his scheming call

Esther planned a banquet and invited the king and Haman
to attend it on that particular day
During the feast, the king asked Esther what she really
wanted, that she could have her way
But she simply invited the king and Haman to another
banquet which she would prepare
Then unable to sleep, flipping through archives, the king
was shocked at his findings there

In the royal archives he read of the assassination plot
Mordecai had foiled sometime before
And was amazed that Mordecai had never been rewarded
for this awesome deed furthermore
So when the king asked Haman how a hero should be
shown distinguished appreciation
Haman thought the king was referring to him, so he
suggested a generous commendation

The king agreed, but Haman was mortified when he learned
Mordecai was to be the honoree
During the second banquet, when the king asked Esther her
desire, she made an earnest plea
There was a plot to destroy her and her people, and she
named Haman the culprit and then
The king ordered Haman hanged on the same gallows he
had built for Mordecai's end

Then Mordecai was promoted to Haman's position, and the
king's ring sealed the news
The king granted Esther and Mordecai the right to avert any
plan that endangered the Jews
They were ensured protection throughout the province and
how joyfully they celebrated!
Because of the faith and courage of Esther and her devoted
cousin, a people was extricated

Read Esther and imagine how you might step outside your
expected role and find
That risking life and limbs in order to be used by God is
exquisitely divine
Imagine your life making a difference, so seize each
moment and don't resist
Let Him use you today, for perhaps He has called *you* to act
in such a time as this

JOB

After Job had prayed for his friends,
the LORD made him prosperous again
and gave him twice as much as he had before.
42:10

JOB

Job was a wealthy and honorable man whose love for God
would never depart
He was concerned that perhaps his sons had sinned and
cursed God in their hearts
So he would offer sacrifices to God to ask for forgiveness
for all their sins
Which shows he cared for his children's spiritual health
with a faithful regimen

Then one day Satan wished to prove Job's faith wasn't of
God's gracious touch
But only because things were going well and because God
had given him so much
So God permitted Satan to attack Job, causing him to suffer
beyond comprehension
He lost his children, his possessions and health, but
harbored not an iota of dissension

When three of Job's friends heard of the difficulties he
encountered in his adversity
They came to sympathize and to comfort him as friends
ought to do naturally
When they saw his great pain, they wept and didn't speak
for seven days and nights
But then argued that Job's suffering was a result of sin and
he should make it right

Though frustration and lamentation took hold, Job
professed his conscience was clear
Declaring his friends had misconstrued the reason for his
suffering, so he persevered
After young Elihu, with a different view, contended that
suffering is meant as a remedy
God finally responded and Job repented for questioning
God's power and sovereignty

Job beseeched God to explain and bring relief, but no
answer was received at all
Instead He answered Job with the revelation of His
creation, to renew and to enthrall
Then God rebuked Job's friends for assuming his suffering
was due to sin ignored
And reinstated Job's fortunes and granted him even greater
blessings than before

Certainly it can happen that suffering is not always a
penalty for our sin
And those who obey God have no amnesty from trouble
without or within
Even if we aren't able to fully understand the pain we
might go through
It can lead us toward rediscovering our God and
strengthening our faith, too

Read Job and learn that we must recognize Satan's tactics
and his itinerancy
But we should never let him come between us and our
Lord, no matter the tragedy
Read Job and learn though sometimes He may appear
distant, God is always near
So when we feel alone, helpless or in distress, never doubt,
question or fear

Read Job and learn that when all else has vanished, God is
all we need
He doesn't have to explain anything for His faithfulness is
guaranteed
Read Job and learn that we must hold onto God with every
ounce of our ability
And remember that with all life's trials and woes, this isn't
our final destiny

Read Job and make a decision to submit to God's sovereignty
No matter what happens in our fragile lives, trust Him
explicitly

PSALMS

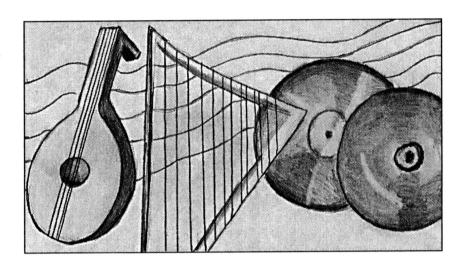

Let everything that has breath praise the LORD.
Praise the LORD!
150:6

PSALMS

The psalmists praised and worshiped God and confessed all
sorts of iniquities
Their true feelings were poured out in song and prayer for
hope or perplexities
First, the psalmists praised God for His justice and cited
trust in His mercy and love
Then they recalled the corruption of man and begged for
forgiveness from above

They asked God to liberate them from their enemies here,
there and everywhere
And related how the sinners who begged forgiveness were
joyous beyond compare
They depicted God as a shepherd whose love abounds in
spite of man's atrocious sin
And conveyed how one's sorrow for sin can offer a chance
to start all over again

In Psalms there is prayer for deliverance and a call to
worship our God the King
There are sins confessed and tremendous urgings to trust in
the Lord in everything
There's a psalm for those who've been deceived and
wounded by a friend
And prayer to the Almighty for those who have been
slandered without end

Other psalms praise the omnipotence of God who alone is
perfection proclaimed
And cite lessons to be learned from Jewish history—from
slavery to David's reign
Behold God's faithfulness and promise to David—the same
as He promises today
And there's a distinct urgency to continually worship the
Lord and to faithfully pray

There's a prayer of Moses, the oldest of the psalmists, with
deep poetic expression
In which he advises that life is short and our time should be
used with wise discretion
One psalm tells about persecutors of others, many glorify
God who sets forth delivery
There are psalms of repentance and of how God delivers in
spite of our selfish tendency

The psalms praise and thank God, recalling blessings
received when we live righteously
They nudge and provoke us to perceive that the greatest
sacrifice to God is this recipe:
Faith and obedience to Him in every nook and cranny or
spotlight of our existence
Showing us that ultimately God's path is the right one, no
matter the obstacles or distance

Psalms, written by David and others, known and unknown
authors of inspiring poetry
From the pit of despair to the pinnacle of celebration, they
cry, they sing in misery or glee
But crying or rejoicing, they convey their honesty with
God, their bona fide and best friend
Psalms offers jubilation, comfort and peace in times of
trials—a prescription to heal, to mend

Read the book of Psalms and let it lead you straight into
God's awesome direction
Let it guide you into an authentic relationship with Him, let
Him be your true protection
Use the psalms for singing and praying in worship, to
praise and thank God for His Word
Grasp His trust and power, His justice and mercy with an
honesty waiting to be heard

Read Psalms and let your heart sing!
Read Psalms and worship the King!

PROVERBS

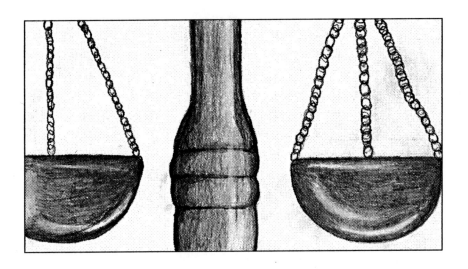

The fear of the LORD is the beginning of knowledge,
but fools despise wisdom and discipline.
1:7

Trust in the LORD with all your heart
And do not lean on your own understanding.
In all your ways acknowledge Him,
And He will make your path straight.
3:5-6

PROVERBS

Solomon, who wrote most of Proverbs, teaches how to gain
wisdom and discreet living
How to attain discipline and do what's impartial, what's
right and what's forgiving
How to apply our knowledge to everyday life, doing what is
just and morally okay
It imparts moral truth and a practical compilation of wise
words for everyday

There is fatherly advice for young people with wise words
for living righteously
You'll see that a know-it-all is a fool, for only God is the
know-it-all authority
And even when sin feels good, it is still deadly and is only
short-range pleasure
So avoid people who wish to entice us into sin, for it's
ungodly beyond measure

When we lack wisdom, we are utterly unable to distinguish
right from wrong
But God will pour out His Holy Spirit in us if we heed His
beseeching song
Those lacking wisdom are rebellious and foolish, and don't
seek it earnestly
But if we seek and find wisdom, though laborious, it will
bring endless security

Wisdom is turning every inch of our life over to God for
guidance in all we do
Wisdom is always giving to God first from whatever is
earned or from gifted revenue
Wise parents will pass on their wisdom to the children from
generation to generation
Teaching that seeking God's wisdom must be first choice—
the primary consideration

The wise man acts in a responsible way so that his family
isn't punished or distressed
He doesn't yield to temptation or laziness, doesn't shun
work or relish sleep in excess
The wise man doesn't break God's law, but opposes sexual
sin or other selfish desires
So heed the warning against self-destruction due to foolery,
and submit as He requires

Don't keep hateful feelings inside; admit them and ask God
to make them disappear
Seek those who speak truth even if it hurts, not those who
tell you what you want to hear
A wise person models a meaningful life and attracts those
seeking that same life, too
And because of the wisdom gained, we can lead others to
God and let salvation ensue

Those who respond to criticism with accepting correction
gain wisdom and grow from it
And those who are really brave don't look for opportunities
to prove their wit and grit
Whenever we're about to do a good deed only because we
want something in return
We must ask ourselves if God would be pleased with our
self-serving concern

Alcohol, like other drugs, blurs the mind—leads to sin,
poor decisions and shattered lives
And those who make mistakes repeatedly but refuse advice
will soon see disaster arrive
The wise man doesn't refuse God's call or reject His
command to be faithful and obey
The wise man doesn't wish to face consequences, doesn't
want God to turn him away

Prepare for temptation now by settling on exactly how
you'll act when you encounter it
For it's easier to resist if you've decided beforehand you
won't give in, you won't submit
If you have no aim or direction, there's instability and
vulnerability to temptation
So make sure your life is filled with the Word and
wisdom—with godly participation

These are only a few examples of various life matters and
wisdom for godly application
Proverbs offers even more practical wisdom for daily living
as a road to liberation
It provides you with thoughts and lessons on discipline,
truth, marriage and self-control
On wealth, poverty, family life, gossip, God's heart, and
there's more to behold

Read Proverbs and follow the common sense advice
Of appropriate lessons of danger signs, truth and sacrifice
Read Proverbs and apply truths for managing each day
Know that God—wisdom's source—will never turn away

You should not read these proverbs as mere fact
But live out what you learn; read and then act
Read! Reflect and connect!
Read! Apply and—swhoosh! Fly!!!

ECCLESIASTES

*All that my eyes desired I did not refuse them.
I did not withhold my heart from any pleasure...
and behold all was vanity and striving after wind
and there was no profit under the sun.*
2:10a, 11b

*The conclusion, when all has been heard, is:
fear God and keep His commandments,
because this applies to every person.*
12:13

ECCLESIASTES

Ecclesiastes sketches Solomon's life and its true meaning is
brought forth and analyzed
Solomon reflects on every phase he had previously
undertaken, sampled or scrutinized
He recalls how everything had been thoughtless, idiotic and
empty—an exercise in futility
This from a man who had it all—wisdom, power, wealth—
yet spiraled downhill aimlessly

As the story goes, Solomon asked God for Wisdom and
became the wisest man on earth
He studied, he taught, he judged, he penned, and leaders
from other nations knew his worth
So they came to Jerusalem to learn from him, hoping they
would become just as wise as he
But with all of his wisdom, Solomon ultimately failed to
heed his own advice faithfully

Nearing his end, Solomon looks back over his life and is
exceedingly dissatisfied
Showing us that clutching and grabbing for worldly
pleasures can lead to emptiness inside
He endeavors to free us from snatching and clawing for
power, money, and self-validation
And helps us to discover that life is empty apart from God,
apart from His transformation

Some pleasures pursued by Solomon were evil and some
were honorable accomplishments
But even the honorable pursuits were useless when he
pursued them as fleshly fulfillment
For he didn't look past the deeds to reasons for doing them
and the intentions they rendered
His aim in life should have been to seek God as the source
for purpose, all in His splendor

Solomon observes that timing is of great importance, that
there is a time for everything
Gain knowledge, but obey and respect God's timing—let
the peace fall which He brings
Solomon further observes that man has a spiritual thirst
which only eternity can satisfy
That man should fear God and always make him first in life
without a single alibi

It's foolish to make a promise you cannot keep or even
half-way fulfill a particular vow
It's much better not to promise than to make a promise to
God and then break it somehow
Solomon notes that money in itself is not evil, but the love
of money leads to sinful stuff
And if you depend on money for happiness, most certainly
you'll never have quite enough

God allows us to experience good times and bad times
which is part of everyone's plight
And doesn't allow us to foresee the future or rely on our
own understanding or might
Generally, we're inclined to take credit for all the good
times which subtly sashay our way
But will blame God for the bad times we endure which
often arise out of our going astray

Solomon continues and clearly warns us that there is one
fate for each and everyone
That after death, you can't return and change all the wrong
things you have done
That life without God can generate a bitter, lonely and
empty old-age existence
So draw close to God in your youth; passing pleasures can
be detours creating distance

Read Ecclesiastes and see that Solomon isn't trying to
destroy our hope, our expectation
Rather, he guides us to the only one who can offer meaning
to life through salvation
Read Ecclesiastes and listen to Solomon's warning, his
great foresight and prophecy
Then commit to living for God because apart from Him life
is empty, a story of futility

SONG OF SOLOMON

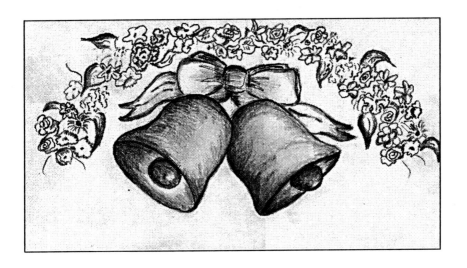

"I am my beloved's and my beloved is mine,
He who pastures his flock among the lilies."
6:3

SONG OF SOLOMON

The Song of Solomon is a song of love, honoring marriage
between male and female
Solomon sees her working in a royal vineyard and tries to
meet her, but to no avail
But later, disguised as a shepherd, he returns to the peasant
tending her vines
Then wins her love, reveals his true identity and their
courtship begins to shine

An ordinary Jewish maiden and a king express their strong
feelings for one another
With dialogue of love, giving words of their longing to be
together with each other
They desire to rid themselves of what could cause problems
and hinder their relationship
For little problems should not be shrugged off and ignored,
but handled with a steady grip

Solomon proposes and she accepts—remaining a virgin as
God would have both be
Then finally their wedding day arrives and they are married
in holy matrimony
Their marriage grows in spite of problems, but she becomes
tepid toward him one day
And by the time she recovers and is ready to respond,
Solomon has gone astray

She quickly begins searching for him because she is
tormented by their separation
And later she articulates her respect for him—her
beloved—and her appreciation
Then both convey delight in each other and Solomon
declares admiration for his bride
How priceless is love approved by God and shared within
the boundaries He sanctified

Read Song of Solomon and recognize that devotion and
commitment in marriage is key
Just as our relationship with God should demonstrate our
faithfulness unmistakably
Singles all, honor God—honor yourselves, your beloved
and God's moral objectives
Stand firm against sexual temptation and commit to
viewing sex from God's perspective

Read Song of Solomon and recognize that marriage must
be refreshed every now and then
Concentrate on your spouse's strengths, the covenanted
wedding vows and circumvent sin
As the church—His faithful followers—is Christ's bride
whom He loves unconditionally
So an earthly marriage should reflect God's love and your
commitment in holy matrimony

ISAIAH

But He was pierced through for our transgressions,
He was crushed for our iniquities;
The chastening for our well-being fell upon Him,
And by His scourging we are healed.
53:5

ISAIAH

Isaiah was commissioned to be God's messenger through a
vision of God sitting upon a throne
The angels spoke and rather than blessings, Isaiah had to
tell his people God would destroy His own
Then Isaiah realized he too was unclean and could see no
hope of measuring up to God's perfection
So after a painful process of cleansing, his sins were
forgiven and he submitted to God's direction

Isaiah, a great prophet, was used by God to speak to Judah,
Israel and surrounding pagan nations
He summoned the people to repent, warning them of God's
judgment and disciplining situations
But they were unwilling to follow God completely, even
abandoned loyal sacrifices at holy rites
They wouldn't relinquish the unfaithfulness consuming
their hearts, so unrighteous in God's sight

In both Israel and Judah, idol worshiping flourished under
the reign of evil kings and evil done
A few good kings tamed it during their reign, but God's day
of reckoning marked the sinful ones
He would siege Jerusalem and destroy her leaders, the first
to receive God's mighty judgment
Judging both good and evil—the proud humbled, the lofty
brought down—that was His intent

The women of Judah dressed to be noticed, to be
fashionable to gain special approval from man
They placed emphasis on clothing and jewelry rather than
on God who holds the master plan
They ignored God's purpose for their lives, ignored the
poor wallowing in great oppression
Self-centered and self-serving, they flaunted blessings from
God and abused their possessions

During the suffering, Isaiah had predicted God would protect
a remnant with His loving grace
The protected will be set apart unto God for the time when
the Messiah rules this earthly place
Their signature will not be riches, power, prestige, fame or
such, but a holiness designation
Deriving from sincerity in obedience to God, from
ungrudging devotion in godly relations

Despite Israel's spiritual collapse, God will show them
mercy and deliver them from captivity
Then restore them with love—not wrath—though His heart
wept for their rebellion sorrowfully
God used other nations to punish Israel, but afterward
redeemed her—calling her by name
And reminded Israel she was to be a witness, His power
and deeds to the world to proclaim

God's judgment for sin upon the entire world was issued
forth as His sovereignty directed
Then Isaiah praised God for working wonders which were
awesome, complete and perfected
Repeatedly, words of hope came, anticipating the wondrous
coming of the Messiah for all men
A suffering servant and a sovereign Lord, he foretold God's
sacrifice for our repetitive sin

The prophecy revealed the Messiah's appearance would not
be viewed as pleasing to the eye
This man of sorrows would be despised, rejected by men
who'd refuse to laud and magnify
God allowed His people to look to the future, to Jesus'
suffering and saving the world's lost
For like sheep we stray from God, we go our own way, so
He'd nail all our sins onto the cross

Because of Isaiah's passion for Israel and his desire to see
them close to their LORD above
He prayed that God would save her from her rotten sin, and
would grant mercy in His love
He is merciful to His people who are humble and repentant,
who reveres His Word honestly
But He punishes those who are prideful and stray, whose
sacrifice is deceptive compliancy

Read Isaiah and meet a strong and valiant man of God
proclaiming His holy Word
Heed his message, repent and be renewed—seek Christ and
let your heart be stirred
Read Isaiah and meet God with promises of comfort,
deliverance and restoration
Of the Messiah reigning over His flock and coming again
to complete our salvation

Read Isaiah and see the unfaithful doomed with a grave
portrait of God's judgment
But for the faithful there is a splendid and priceless
reward—an eternal testament
Read Isaiah and wonder why—like the Israelites—you
ignore God, rebelling repeatedly
And why all of humanity wouldn't want to be God's eager,
obedient and willing devotee

JEREMIAH

"Only acknowledge your iniquity,
That you have transgressed against the LORD your God.
3:13a

"For I know the plans I have for you," declares the
LORD,
"plans to prosper you and not to harm you,
plans to give you hope and a future."
29:11

JEREMIAH

It was a chaotic time as Babylon, Egypt and Assyria
contended for world dominancy
And Judah was wedged in the middle of the political
confusion and in immorality
So God appointed Jeremiah as prophet to Judah during the
reign of her last five kings
And Jeremiah devotedly confronted the people about their
sin and judgment's sting

Jeremiah reminded them of God's faithfulness to make sure
they wouldn't forget
He stressed God's eternal love for them as he recited
Israel's history, specifying their debt
He reminded them of the time when they were close to
God, a people holy and dedicated
And now they had forsaken Him to worship idols rather
than Living Water consecrated

Jeremiah condemned Judah for its love for idols, her awful
unfaithfulness revealed
Seeking security in uncertain things rather than in God
whose love is forever sealed
Judah's sin spots were more than superficial and couldn't
be cleansed with soap or lye
Only God alone could remove the stains if they would
allow Him to purge and rectify

Even though Israel had fallen to Assyria and the people
were taken into captivity
The painful lesson of their fall should have caused Judah to
heed God's warning willingly
But Judah gave no thought to God, refused to repent—
ignoring Jeremiah's prognostications
Ignored his prophecy of coming disaster, which could have
saved the people from eradication

Jeremiah predicted a day would come when the two nations
would be reunited as one at last
When they would see sin as sin and restore true worship of
God, sincere and steadfast
But now Jeremiah was distressed over the certain
devastation of their approaching judgment
It would persist until the people disposed of sin and obeyed
God, silencing the consequence

The men of Judah thought they could get away with their
countless sins of idolatry
If they came to the temple and said, "We are delivered!"—
an insult uttered negligently
For polluting the temple with human sacrifices, God would
curse it just like Shiloh
He desires obedience, not rituals; a vessel of sacrifice
minus commitment is worthless cargo

Jeremiah was weary of watching Judah's unholy
ceremonial substitute for God's mandate
So he wept over her sin and her ensuing punishment,
hoping she'd repent before too late
The flesh strives for earthly wisdom, power and riches—
characteristics humans admire
But God delights in lovingkindness, justice and
righteousness—these traits He does require

Pashhur, the priest, caused Jeremiah to be beaten and jailed
when he heard him prophesying
When released, Jeremiah issued doom to Pashhur,
Jerusalem and Judah, all who were defying
He prophesied against king after king and warned
Jerusalem of her present impending fall
He contrasted the corrupt rulers with the coming Messiah,
who would come to reign over all

Jeremiah continued to prophesy, to warn the people to
repent or face certain destruction
The priests and false prophets became incensed, threatening
death after his abduction
But the elders spared Jeremiah and he plugged along,
repeating his message to repent
The people defended him, for he had spoken in the name of
the LORD with godly intent

God punished the people of Judah by appointing a
foreigner to come along and weigh in
Nebuchadnezzar was not sent to proclaim God, but to
assign judgment on Judah's sin
So Jeremiah entreated Zedekiah to surrender to Babylon's
king rather than stand and fight
To dismiss false prophets, but serve the king and live
obediently in God's sight

Then the Babylonians captured Jerusalem just as Jeremiah
had previously prophesied
And Zedekiah imprisoned Jeremiah for predicting the city
would be captured and occupied
While the king teetered between public opinion and God's
will, surrender and resistance
An order was given for Jeremiah's release from prison at
Nebuchadnezzar's insistence

He also prophesied against Gentile nations; upon them
God's judgment he did foretell
Just as Jerusalem had received her punishment, these
nations would receive theirs as well
They would also fall because of sin—such as idolatry,
selfishness, thievery and pride
They were responsible for their own ruin since refusing
truth made God dissatisfied

Jeremiah lived to see his prophesies of destruction and
captivity definitely fulfilled
Judah's sin resulted in her bondage for seventy years in
exile—all which God revealed
Jeremiah was allowed to stay there and he advised the
remaining Judeans not to flee
Disobeying, they fled to Egypt, forcing him to go—where
he might have died eventually

Read Jeremiah and discover a man who appeared
unsuccessful in the world's eye
Possessing no money, family or friends, but was blessed
with the gift to prophesy
Though political and religious leaders and the people
refused to accept his advice
We see he completed the task God gave him and that would
more than suffice

Read Jeremiah and discover that success can't be measured
by fame, fortune or popularity
For these are temporal measures that are too often used as
excuses for sinning repeatedly
God measures our success by our obedience, by our faith
and by our righteousness
And His approval alone should be our standard for service,
our standard for success

Do God's work even if you must suffer, be taunted or
rejected
Embrace Jeremiah's faith and courage and then be God-
directed

LAMENTATIONS

My eyes fail because of tears,
My spirit is greatly troubled;
My heart is poured out on the earth
Because of the destruction of the daughter of my people,
When little ones and infants faint
In the streets of the city.
2:11

LAMENTATIONS

Lamentations is Jeremiah's song of sorrow for Jerusalem's
destruction
A defeated nation, a destroyed temple, an exiled people by
abduction
He wept because the people had rejected God and
witnessed desolation
He wept because God had to reject their rebellion, their
insubordination

Rather than being elated over the fact that God had fulfilled
His prophesy
He wept bitterly for his people who had abandoned God,
causing great misery
For people who had sought assistance and protection from
other nations instead
Who played with fire and got burned, refusing to believe
God's judgment ahead

The Judeans confessed that the Lord was just in sending
them into captivity
And then prayed that God would repay the evilness of their
crowing enemies
Admitting their transgressions, their perpetual complaining
and faintheartedness
They realized their circumstance, yet found God's
everlasting mercy nevertheless

Jeremiah saw God's compassion as a new day and his
faithfulness ever so great
He took his eyes off himself and onto the Lord and saw it
was good to quietly wait
He waited for the salvation of the Lord; each lesson he
willingly wanted to learn
He saw that God's chastisement should be accepted and the
bad egg repent and return

God saw Jerusalem's sin greater than the sin of Sodom—
God's definitive judgment
Where priests and prophets should have upheld the
temple's purity by being diligent
Instead they spread evil and corruption, leading the people
into sin and final devastation
Refusing to listen to Jeremiah and rely on God resulted in
their ultimate ruination

Jeremiah lamented over the people's forced labor and high
cost for necessities
For oppression, famine and danger, and multitudes
experiencing explicit atrocities
For hardships to young men, boys and elders, for joy of the
heart that ceased
Again Jeremiah prayed for mercy for the people, for
restoration and release

Read Lamentations and behold Judah's suffering, all
because of sin
Though God shunned them, He didn't abandon them—but
He disciplined
Despite their sinfulness in the past, He would restore them
if they would return
Because their hope was entrenched in the LORD—a lesson
we all should learn

Read Lamentations and behold Jeremiah's tears as unselfish
tears he cried
Tears over a people greatly blessed by God, yet whom time
and again they defied
Read Lamentations and behold that in our troubles and
grief, hope springs anew
Oh, how God suffers when we suffer; oh, how our sin
breaks His heart in two!

EZEKIEL

"For I will take you out of the nations;
I will gather you from all the countries
and bring you back into your own land.
I will sprinkle clean water on you,
and you will be clean;
I will cleanse you from all your impurities
and from all your idols.
I will give you a new heart
and put a new spirit in you;
I will remove from you your heart of stone
and give you a heart of flesh."
36:24-26

EZEKIEL

With thousands of other captives, Ezekiel was carried away
by the Babylonians into exile
Four or five years later, God called him to be a prophet to
Judah, a nation to be reconciled
Due to the people's sins, God would allow Judah to be
destroyed and Jerusalem would fall
But He promised to restore the land to those who remained
faithful to Him throughout it all

When God saw Ezekiel's open and obedient attitude, the
spirit overflowed deeply inside
For God knew Ezekiel would be in need of His power as a
counselor and spiritual guide
He knew his ministry ahead wouldn't be popular, for the
people wouldn't admit their sin
God dubbed them stubborn and obstinate, with rebellion
the great monster living within

Ezekiel had to take God's words to heart before delivering
them to the nation
His message had to sink deep inside and his attitude
confirmed his qualification
So he began the tedious task of prophesying among the
people living in captivity
He warned them of the consequences if they failed to
surrender to God's authority

God gave Ezekiel specific instructions on to what to do,
how to do it and what to say
He commanded Ezekiel to portray the siege of Jerusalem
using a tablet of clay
He had to lie on his left side 390 days for the number of
years of Israel's punishment
And lie on his right side 40 days for the number of years in
prison to be spent

God told Ezekiel to shave his head and beard, prophesying
Jerusalem's desolation
And to divide his hair into thirds to represent the fate of the
people—their devastation
One-third would die by fire; one-third would fall by the
sword in the city throughout
And one-third would be exiled to other nations, to foreign
winds around and about

Then God directed Ezekiel to put a few strands of hair in
his garment to symbolize
The small amount of faithful ones who would be spared,
whom God would recognize
But even some of this remnant would be judged because of
faith which was not real
And so later on would also perish for the wickedness
displayed, for their sinful ordeal

Ezekiel prophesied that idolatry would call down God's
ultimate wrath and judgment
That the destruction would be complete, not for revenge,
but to ensure that truth be sent
For Judah trusted in her prosperity, possessions and such—
not in the Lord instead
So her pride would be crushed and peace would slumber—
only havoc, only dread

God assured the people He'd continue being their God, no
matter where they might be
Concerning exiles in Babylonia, His promise would prevail
throughout their captivity
He promised to restore the faithful few to Jerusalem, the
home they had left behind
But in the meantime, God would be their sanctuary and
transform hearts and minds

Evil rulers would be judged, false prophets and idolatrous
elders would be condemned
Alas! The city would not be spared, for God would never
break His promise to them
If the people repented, He would forgive them and renew
His covenant once again
So that they might *remember and be ashamed* of all their
wretchedness, all their sin

When Ezekiel's wife died, he wasn't allowed to mourn, he
wasn't allowed to weep
For God had instructed him that tears must not come, that
there should be no grief
To signify to fellow exiles that they were not to mourn over
Jerusalem's desolation
Once prophecies had come to pass, Ezekiel's restriction
would come to termination

God also brought judgment upon the Gentile nations
surrounding Judah's principality
The judgment was not simply a vindictive declaration of
Jews against their enemies
Rather, judgment upon nations that refused to acknowledge
God as being supreme
Who failed to fulfill one righteous purpose God intended,
the purpose to redeem

Finally, Ezekiel prophesied on the restoration and reunion
of the divided nation
And reminded Israel and Judah when they repented of their
sins in godly declaration
The temple would then be rebuilt and the LORD'S light
would return in all of its glory
God would fill them with His Spirit and lay bare the
Messiah's blessed ransom story

Read Ezekiel and discover that when we focus on God,
turn and confess
He will give us the power needed to defeat sin, reflecting
His holiness
Read Ezekiel and discover God, who is truth and perfection,
can equip us to live
Far beyond our tendency to compromise with the world
and, yes, He will forgive

Read Ezekiel and discover we must be faithful to God, not
just for what He can do
But because we love Him in times of prosperity and in
times of tribulations, too
If we desire to be like Christ, we must be devoted to Him
with more than just our talk
And when God calls, we must obey—making any sacrifice
necessary in our walk

Read Ezekiel and discover through regular worship we
learn of change needed within
We can be restored to perfect fellowship with God and each
other if we deal with our sin

DANIEL

"It is He who changes the times and the epochs;
He removes kings and establishes kings;
He gives wisdom to wise men
And knowledge to men of understanding.
It is He who reveals the profound and hidden things;
He knows what is in the darkness,
And the light dwells with Him."
2:21-22

DANIEL

When Nebuchadnezzar invaded Jerusalem, he took
multitudes into captivity
Among those, Daniel, Hananiah, Mishael and Azariah
entered his royal family
After training for three years, they entered the king's
personal service as arranged
Were given new names of Belteshazzaar, Shadrach,
Meshach and Abed-nego, the change

They were allowed a daily ration of choice foods and wine
to drink, all from the king
But Daniel resolved he would not defile himself by
accepting any of those things
So he sought permission for him and his friends to have
vegetables and water instead
After negotiating and ten days of testing, they were
healthier than youth otherwise fed

Hence, they were accepted by the king and were ten times
better than others who attended
For God had gifted them with knowledge and wisdom on
which the king depended
To Daniel He had granted understanding in visions and
dreams—a God-given ability
And when the king's wise men couldn't interpret his dream,
death to them was his decree

Daniel didn't panic, but requested extra time to reveal the
dream's interpretation
Then he found his three friends and prayed to the Lord
concerning this serious situation
Daniel's prayer was answered when the mystery of the
dream appeared in a night vision
So he took time to give credit and thank God for wisdom
and for answering his petition

When Daniel arrived before the king, he did not take credit
for this unique ability
But gave the honor and glory to God alone as he explained
the dream's mystery
He also gave his three friends credit when he presented the
dream's interpretation
Pointing people to God, to Him the glory, seeing needs of
others—not self-preservation

Then the king honored Daniel and God, making him ruler
over Babylon and his wise men
And Daniel appointed Shadrach, Meshach and Abed-nego
over the administration therein
Afterward, the king made an idolatrous and lofty image of
gold and set it upon the plain
He commanded all to fall down and worship it whenever
music was heard in the domain

Any who refused would be cast into the midst of a furnace
of blazing fire immediately
But Shadrach, Meshach and Abed-nego refused to worship
the idol—hail those trusting three!
When given one more chance to worship the idol and deny
God and His awesome might
They still chose to stay faithful to God, regardless of the
consequences or their plight

Due to its excessive heat, the men who threw them into the
furnace were killed instantly
But when King Nebuchadnezzar looked into the fire, he
saw four instead of three
The king was so impressed with how the men were saved
from being touched by the flames
Until he acknowledged God's power and forbade anyone to
speak against God's name

Later the king had another dream which was of a tree so
beautiful, fruitful and high
That spread to the ends of all the earth with a Holy One
descending from the sky
And ordered the tree chopped down and the king became a
wild beast for seven years
So after Daniel had heard this dream, he revealed its
meaning to the king's royal ears

The dream meant that the king would lose his throne and
for seven years be insane
Living like an animal in the field—not destroyed, but
restored as Daniel explained
Then Daniel pleaded with the king to change and God gave
him a year to repent
Unwisely, after a year passed with no repentance, his time
had been fully spent

Thus the dream was fulfilled and it came to pass that for
seven years he lived like a beast
At the end of that time, he turned and acknowledged God's
power would never cease
That He was the Most High who lives forever, so he praised
God—exalted and glorified
Then Nebuchadnezzar was restored to his kingdom, for
God had humbled his ghastly pride

When Belshazzar ruled after Nebuchadnezzar, Daniel
interpreted handwriting on the wall
It predicted Babylon would be divided between the Medes
and Persians, saying it would fall
The prediction came true that same night when armies
marched in and slew the king
They seized Babylon; then Darius the Mede became king
with world dominion in full swing

Daniel became one of Darius' top advisors and the king
planned to promote him as head
Jealous officials found nothing to criticize, so they attacked
Daniel's religion instead
They persuaded the king to pass a law forbidding praying
to God, with a harsh penalty
But Daniel continued praying routinely three times a day
and was reported by his enemies

The law was not alterable, so Daniel was cast into the lion's
den and spoken to by the king
He assured Daniel that his God would save him; then
sealed the cover with his signet ring
When the king arose at dawn, he rushed to the lion's den
and saw Daniel had been protected
For his faith never wavered and through the angel God sent,
Daniel was delivered as directed

Daniel himself had dreams and visions dealing with the
future which he didn't understand
One dream presented a prophecy of God's redemption, of
the Messiah coming to rescue man
Another revealed the rejection and death of Christ by His
own, a perfect kingdom prediction
God's grace imparted to sinful man will come through
Jesus and His sacrificial crucifixion

Read Daniel and see that only God is in control of our
destiny
That if we trust Him, He'll give us direction and bring
tranquility
Tenacity is necessary to keep the faith alive without
compromise
Not allowing our walk to become foggy, humdrum or
anesthetized

Read Daniel and see that we should be persistent in our
integrity and prayer
Being content to serve God no matter the calling, no matter
when or where
Just trust in Him and watch Him deliver you from your
trials or tribulations
Yield not to pressures of sin around you, yield not to life's
temptations

HOSEA

Then the LORD said to me,
"Go, show your love to your wife again,
though she is loved by another
and is an adulteress.
Love her as the LORD loves the Israelites,
though they turn to other gods
and love the sacred raisin cakes."
3:1

HOSEA

Hosea focuses on the parallels between his relationship
with his adulterous wife
And God's relationship with the northern kingdom of Israel
and her sinful life
Israel pursued false gods after making a covenant with
God, exalted and magnified
It's a love story of a man and his wife and of God's love for
His people, His bride

God commanded Hosea to marry Gomer, a woman who
would cause him heartache
Who would be unfaithful and then abandon Hosea for
lust—and how she did forsake!
But Hosea searched for her, found her and redeemed her,
and brought her home again
Because he loved her, they reconciled—like God's mercy to
Israel—despite her sin

God wanted Israel to turn from sin and worship Him
alone—the only righteous way
But the nation disobeyed and was consumed with tons of
moral and spiritual decay
The people willfully ignored God, and so their sin would
result in their desolation
Just as Gomer didn't grasp Hosea's love, Israel snubbed
God's love and lamentation

Hosea also warned Judah against following Israel's
rebellious and sinful style
But Judah broke the covenant, forgot her God, and
experienced invasion and exile
Just as Hosea sought his adulterous wife, brought her back
and forgave her sin
The LORD seeks us with His love—gentle and faithful—so
we can start over again

Read Hosea and notice God's loyalty and eternal love
seated in devotion
And like the prophet, we must willingly submit—a holy
priority notion
Read Hosea and notice God's message and revel awhile in
His piety
For if you refuse to choose His path, you'll lose your way
repeatedly

Read Hosea and notice—like Gomer—we can chase the
traps of secular pleasure
Such as power, money, prestige, lust—all worldly
temptations, all worldly treasures
Read Hosea and notice that rebellion toward God is sure to
result in disaster
And if we rebel and disobey, no blessings will flow from
our exalted Master

JOEL

"Yet even now," declares the LORD,
Return to Me with all your heart,
And with fasting, weeping and mourning;
And rend your heart and not your garments."
Now return to the LORD your God,
For He is gracious and compassionate,
Slow to anger, abounding in lovingkindness
And relenting of evil.
2:12-13

JOEL

God urged all parents to pass their history down to the
children, generation to generation
Relating repeatedly to them important lessons learned, to
ensure their spiritual maturation
When a locust plague was predicted to invade the land, to
bring destruction cloaked in agony
It was like a prophecy of God's punishment for sin, Judah's
dreadful condemnation debris

Joel urged the people to return to God before an even
greater catastrophe occurred
Because without God, destruction is a certainty, with a
ravage never before heard
Joel described the disastrous effects of the plague, saying
the crisis is surely at hand
Warning that an even greater crisis would befall them if
they rejected God's command

Later Joel advised that tearing their garments is only for
remorse of sin they impart
There must be true inner repentance—an attitude toward
God, a tearing of the heart
Then Joel prophesied about God's grace—forgiveness for
sin, His blessings abundantly
But only if the people begin living as God charges,
relinquishing their blatant iniquity

Besides Judah and Israel, judgment warnings were issued
to other surrounding nations
The last word will be God's whose dominion will be
manifest at the world's termination
But along with the message of judgment impending and the
necessity for people to repent
Is God's compassion and promised blessings of deliverance
for the faithful and obedient

Read Joel and observe God's awesome power, His
compassion and His might
His definitive judgment of sin when we ignore good,
suffocating in what's not right
Read Joel and observe the danger of living apart from God,
our heavenly Creator
He solemnly declares there's still time to be saved by the
Holy Resuscitator

AMOS

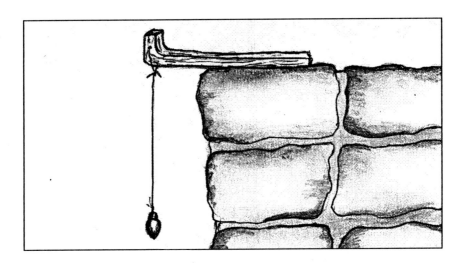

*"But let justice roll down like waters
And righteousness like an ever-flowing stream."
5:24*

AMOS

God sent Amos, a shepherd and fig tree tender, as prophet
to Israel because she fell
To denounce the sins of those surrounding nations and the
sins of Judah as well
The Israelites were powerful and prosperous, but spiritually
tainted throughout
They were greedy, obstinate and unjust, yet went around
pretending to be devout

In Genesis, God chose Israel as the people through whom
He would be proclaimed
Not because they deserved special attention, but to be His
disciples and sow His name
But since they hoarded too much pride and arrogance in
their lofty privileged position
It ruined their sensitivity to God's will and to the spiritual
growth of others' condition

When Amos enumerated and described Israel's hideous
sins, listing them respectively
Amaziah the priest interrupted, trying to halt his preaching
on the spot and permanently
Still Amos continued fearlessly to relate God's message of
Israel's future punishment
And revealed how God would eventually redeem them if
they were faithful and obedient

Read Amos and see that everyone must be accountable for
his own iniquities
And those who reject God, then prosper, must still answer
to His truths and decrees
Read Amos and see that if you're more pleased with self
than with God and His call
Remember that life has no meaning apart from Him and
pride will endorse your fall

OBADIAH

*"The day of the LORD is near for all nations.
As you have done, it will be done to you;
your deeds will return upon your own head."*
1:15

OBADIAH

The Edomites—descendants of Esau—were Israel's bitter
and contrary enemies
And Obadiah's prophecy denounced them for malicious
inflictions and controversies
The people of Edom felt secure, were proud and wealthy
and some worldly-wise
But God would heave them from their lofty towers,
humbling without compromise

Instead of helping Judah when Jerusalem was attacked and
in need of humankind
Edom allowed them to be destroyed, even rejoiced and
looted property left behind
But thieves would steal all the Edomites possessed, allies
would deceive and defeat
They'd be destroyed for their wickedness with no mercy
gleaned at God's holy feet

Read Obadiah and note God's judgment to those hostile
toward His sisters and brothers
And how punishment will inevitably visit upon those who
are evil toward one another
Read Obadiah and note how we cannot allow ourselves to
wallow in ghastly pride
Or feel so comfortable with prosperity and our forbidden
walls till we push God aside

JONAH

When God saw their deeds,
that they turned from their wicked way,
then God relented concerning the calamity
which He had declared He would bring upon them.
And He did not do it.
3:10

JONAH

God called Jonah to go to Nineveh, a city full of corruption,
 with oceans of wickedness
To warn the Assyrians to repent or else receive judgment—
 their glaring sins to confess
But Jonah despised the Assyrians, didn't want them
 receiving mercy and be spared
So instead of obeying, he tried running away from God by
 the sea's thoroughfare

While at sea God sent out a mighty wind that pummeled
 and endangered the ship
Then the captain awakened Jonah and they cast lots to see
 who caused this troubled trip
Jonah was revealed as the culprit and they wondered how
 they could ever calm the sea
So Jonah advised them to toss him overboard, indicating it
 was his responsibility

However, they were reluctant to do that; instead, rowed
 laboriously, trying to reach land
But finally they were driven to hurl him overboard because
 the sea took the upper hand
So they threw Jonah into the sea and subsequently the
 waters subdued the turbulent fight
Then a great fish swallowed him and he was captive in its
 stomach three days and nights

Jonah prayed to God with an abundance of thanksgiving,
remorse and rededication
Remembering God with gratitude, with tremendous praise
and utter glorification
Afterwards, God delivered Jonah from the great fish and his
escape generated prayer
Jonah was given a second chance and willingly obeyed and
fulfilled his mission affair

That pagan city listened and then repented after hearing
God's message only one time
So God canceled His threatened punishment, forgiving
Nineveh for her sinful decline
Now Jonah became angry that his enemies had been spared
and asked that he might die
But God was patient, using a plant, a worm and wind to
stroke his conscience to rectify

Read Jonah and learn that saying no to God only leads to
loads of disaster
But saying yes results in understanding Him and His
purpose as our Master
Read Jonah and learn we can't limit our walk to our own
Christian division
Rather, proclaiming God's Word to all the world should be
our holy mission

Read Jonah and be amazed at how God's mercy is available
if only we repent
How we mustn't hold onto self-centeredness, for that
nudges God's discontent
Read Jonah and be amazed at God's patience when we
rebel, with no regret for sin
Accept God's love and loving others will be easier—His
compassion knows no end

MICAH

And He will arise and shepherd His flock
In the strength of the LORD…
He will be great to the ends of the earth.
This One will be our peace.
5:4, 5

He has showed you, O man, what is good.
And what does the LORD require of you?
To act justly and to love mercy
and to walk humbly with your God.
6:8

MICAH

Through Micah, God warned Israel and Judah of severe
approaching punishment
For indulging in oppression, idolatry and empty worship—
God's wrath was imminent
The corrupt ruler, prophets and priests would pay for their
ungodliness, for their gluttony
Yet after the judgment, God would gather the remnants of
Israel back from captivity

Micah denounced those leaders whose responsibility was to
teach right from wrong
Because they had side-stepped the law and given up
righteousness, God's holy song
They were exploiting the people whom they understood
they were given to serve
And their sins caused them to stray, but God would bring
home what they deserved

After treating the people so wretchedly in order to satisfy
their own requisitions
When in trouble, false prophets had the audacity to seek
God, sending up their petitions
Micah was faithful to God and the words God called him to
disperse were proclaimed
Prophesying a time would come when those imposters
would regret their shifty game

But the people were also to blame because they allowed the
corruption to persist
And didn't call upon God for advice and justice, but let the
misery continue to exist
Then Micah prophesied God's promise of a time of peace
and a time of prosperity
And predicted the end of the time of kings, Zedekiah being
the very last that be

He predicted the future birth and birthplace of the Messiah,
his deity and eternity
The promised King would come, though eternal, would
enter into human history
Even in the midst of judgment, God would deliver those
who would repent and obey
Who would faithfully follow Him—being kind, just and
humble, exclusively His way

God called to the people to declare the reason they turned
their face toward idolatry
The reason they had grown weary of worshiping Him after
His endless loyalty
He only requires His people to be just, love kindness and
follow humbly His path
These things bring Him pleasure, so open your heart to
Him and avoid His wrath

Read Micah to see the foolishness of waving a banner of
faith that's downright insincere
To see we should not ask God for help while disregarding
the downtrodden far or near
Or while silently condoning those who oppress and
exploit—doing nothing at all about it
Because such actions or inactions are glaring iniquities
which God does not permit

Read Micah to see that God truly loves the sinner, but
clearly hates the sin
And through Christ we can find peace if only we repent and
start all over again

NAHUM

*The LORD is slow to anger and great in power,
and the LORD will by no means
leave the guilty unpunished.*
1:3a

NAHUM

As commanded by God, Nahum prophesied against
Assyria, a Gentile world power
And rebuked its rampant militarism and tyranny, against its
high and haughty tower
The Assyrians despised Israel's God—infinite and
righteous—who controls it all
Now the capital city had incurred God's wrath and would
experience a mighty fall

About a century earlier, the people of Nineveh had repented
and therefore were spared
After Jonah had delivered messages in the streets as God
had directed to be shared
But generations later, evil raged again and Nahum saw
oncoming doom their fame
Due to murder, social injustice, deceit and such, the
"bloody city' was tagged its name

Nahum prophesied this lofty controlling world power
would face a dire penalty
Because of its great sins, God would bring it to an end and
destroy it irrevocably
God allows no one to take over His reins, to scoff at His
power or slam His control
And anyone who insists on constant arrogance and
resistance, His wrath will unfold

Read Nahum and you'll understand that no one can hide
from God's judgment
Just obey Him and He'll be your refuge which will make
you secure and content
Read Nahum and understand that God rules all, even those
who reject His way
He alone is sovereign over all that exists and offers a path
to eternity today

Read Nahum and feel God's wrath as He disperses
justice—intolerable to sin
Come and decide to live each day with Him as your LORD,
decide to let Him in

HABAKKUK

LORD, I have heard of your fame;
I stand in awe of your deeds, O LORD.
Renew them in our day,
in our time make them known;
in wrath remember mercy.

3:2

HABAKKUK

Habakkuk was distressed and asked God why Judah wasn't
punished for her iniquity
But God replied that He would use the Babylonians to deal
with Judah properly
Then he was appalled, thinking God's choice more wicked
than Judah's sin supply
God responded and said the people of Judah would survive,
the Babylonians would die

The Babylonians would be punished after God had used
them to fulfill His plan
Though the wicked seemed to triumph, in due time
punishment would be at hand
Habakkuk asked God other questions as to His decisions on
the Chaldean kind
God answered and said He would execute His plan in His
appointed time

Then Habakkuk praised God and hailed His perfect light,
His power and His glory
And determined to wait as God commanded, vowing to
trust Him in every category
God promised that the Chaldeans and all sinners would
perish for evil and idolatry
For God is genuine, alive and sovereign—and controls our
lives and our eternity

Read Habakkuk to perceive a new understanding of God's
power and love
And realize that we too can complain and inquire to the
Holy One above
Read Habakkuk to perceive that He wants us to bring our
trials and our doubts
Though His answer may not be what we expect, not what
we were thinking about

Read Habakkuk to perceive that though the world glorifies
evil with sin yet untold
God steps in when the world makes no sense, for He's
omnipotent and always in control

ZEPHANIAH

Seek the LORD,
all you humble of the earth
Who have carried out His ordinances;
Seek righteousness, seek humility.
Perhaps you will be hidden
in the day of the LORD'S anger.
2:3

ZEPHANIAH

The people of Judah made some attempts to repent, but
they showed no sorrow within
They no longer cared about God and His demands for
righteous living, but continued to sin
Because they felt so prosperous, wealthy and secure, they
became proud and complacent
So they were doomed to suffer God's wrath—He was
provoked and extremely impatient

So Zephaniah warned the Judeans, declaring that if they
refused to repent of idolatry
The entire nation, including their most beloved Jerusalem,
would be destroyed totally
The people had also become polytheistic, worshiping both
the LORD and idols of the land
But no other gods shall come before Him; He's the only
God—that's His first command

Through Zephaniah, God rebuked Jerusalem's princes,
judges, prophets and priests
Because they had become callously disobedient and
irresponsible, sinning without cease
The doom of the Gentile nations was also foretold—to the
north, south, east and west
The punishment would also serve as a means for purifying,
for becoming God's very best

Those who were humble and faithful, who turned only to
the LORD and lived righteously
Would escape God's inevitable judgment and find refuge in
His wondrous security
God has no tolerance for pride and self-reliance on earth;
it's not native to the Holy One
But His people should be encouraged for He reigns with
hope of joyful things to come

Read Zephaniah and find that material comforts can make
us complacent and negligent
Being so excessively content without a care can become a
barrier to our commitment
Read Zephaniah and find that God alone is sovereign—
there's no other god to praise
And when we admit our sins to Him, He'll purge us and
renew us in our earthly days

HAGGAI

*"Is it a time for you yourselves
to be living in your paneled houses,
while this house remains a ruin?"*
1:4

HAGGAI

Years earlier, Jerusalem's temple had been destroyed and
the Jews taken into captivity
Finally, King Cyrus decreed they could return home and
rebuild God's house immediately
So they returned to Jerusalem and began rebuilding the
temple, but the job wasn't fulfilled
And for over fifteen years with no further work done,
apathy led to a shameful standstill

The prophet Haggai delivered God's message to encourage
the people back to His desires
And twenty-three days later the people began construction
as God had explicitly required
If they neglected God's will, He'd generate a drought that
would destroy their subsistence
On their grapes, on their olives, on their grain and cattle,
and on all men in existence

As they worked, many became discouraged—the temple
didn't seem as grand as the one of old
But Haggai encouraged them again to be tenacious without
fear, for God was their stronghold
Then God assured them the glory of the temple's future
would be greater than the one before
That He'd grant peace and through repentance and
obedience, He'd prosper them even more

Haggai reminded the people that as long as the temple was
in ruins, they would be unclean
Their work on the temple would not eradicate their sin, but
they must allow God to intervene
He encouraged the workers once more with God's promise
to subdue the Gentile nations
Declaring God would affirm; ensuring again the coming of
a Messiah for sin's exoneration

Read Haggai and always be open to keeping priorities
straight
Don't put personal comforts above God who alone
dominates
Read Haggai and be open to whatever task God gives you
to do
Don't make excuses, just serve Him and He will see you
through

ZECHARIAH

Behold, your king is coming to you;
He is just and endowed with salvation,
Humble, and mounted on a donkey…
And His dominion will be… to the ends of the earth.
9:9b, 10b

"Two parts… will be cut off and perish…
And I will bring the third part through the fire,
Refine them as silver is refined…
And they will say, 'The LORD is my God.' "
13:8, 9

ZECHARIAH

Zechariah was a prophet of the Judeans who had returned
from their Babylonian captivity
He received eight visions which came to him at night; then
he delivered his prophecy
God warned Israel not to be like their forefathers who
reaped punishment for disobeying
But to heed His words and statutes, to be responsible and
repent for their times of straying

One of the night visions foretold the overthrow of Gentile
nations, Israel's noted enemies
Although those nations prospered, it wouldn't last forever;
God would judge their iniquities
Many of the exiles wanted to remain in Babylon with the
security and wealth obtained
But Zechariah urged them to leave since Babylon would be
destroyed as God had explained

Joshua was Israel's high priest when the remnant returned
to Jerusalem to rebuild the wall
Zechariah saw Joshua in a vision all clothed in sin, with
Satan initiating the call
But Joshua's filthy clothes were exchanged for clean
ones—Satan's accusations rejected
Demonstrating God's mercy and His choice to save His
people in spite of sin neglected

God promised to come to live among the people and many
would come to know His way
The coming of Christ, which would be fulfilled, would
bless the whole world one day
He'd be the Branch, the Messiah, who would come to earth
to remove sin once and for all
To point the world toward God and offer forgiveness for
any who stumble or fall

Zechariah's words brought hope to the exiles as they pined
for a temple as grand as before
He proclaimed the Messiah was coming to erase sin in their
lives forever and evermore
Another night vision signified to the people that only
through God would they succeed
Their own might and resources mattered not, because God's
work is not of human deed

Still another vision revealed that everyone is responsible for
his own actions all the time
That offenders would not only be severely punished, but
would be banished and left behind
The last vision disclosed God's judgment and His wrath
over sin within the one it consumes
But He who deserved to wear the crown would come and
save the world from total doom

Again the Word of the LORD came to Zechariah to answer
a question from Bethel town
The people were holding a fast to remember the time
Jerusalem had been taken down
Since Jerusalem was being rebuilt, they asked if they had to
continue their fast customarily
God told them their need for justice and mercy was more
important than fasting would be

The remnant of exiles who returned struggled to survive—
full of discouragement untold
Then came a sign of peace and prosperity on God's good
earth for the young and the old
And through Zechariah, God encouraged the people to
complete the temple with expediency
He set a vision of the future with promises to bless them,
but they too had a responsibility

After the temple was completed, Zechariah imparted
prophecies of Israel's days to come
Pointing to the first and second coming of the Messiah, to
be fulfilled as God's own Son
God promised to reunite and strengthen the Jewish
kingdom because of His compassion
They'd return from countries where they were dispersed,
protected by God in holy fashion

Zechariah foretold God's wrath against the leaders of Judah
for influencing the people to stray
And told how the land would be purged of idols, how false
prophets and evil would fade away
Then God gave victory to the people who'd prevail
gloriously once the Messiah came along
During His arrest and crucifixion, His disciples would
scatter, but a remnant would stay strong

Read Zechariah and learn that only God knows the future,
has controls over everyone
We should never reject our Lord, lead others astray nor
leave His work undone
Read Zechariah and learn that the Messiah came to reign,
came to die for our mortal sin
Come surrender your life to Him today and prepare for the
promise of His coming again

Read Zechariah and learn that though evil still exists, God's
power is ours to share
And we will be delivered if only we are obedient, knowing
heaven awaits us there
Read Zechariah and learn that God alone is our Creator, our
hope and security
So strive each day to humble your heart, strengthen your
faith and secure eternity

MALACHI

" For I, the LORD, do not change;
therefore you, O son of Jacob, are not consumed.
From the days of your fathers
you have turned aside from My statutes
and have not kept them.
Return to Me, and I will return to you,"
says the LORD of hosts.
"But you say, 'How shall we return?' "
3:6-7

MALACHI

Through Malachi, God pleaded His love for Israel, though
they sinned more and more
When they questioned His love, He cited His love for
Jacob, their descendant chosen before
Then He charged the priests with dishonoring Him and not
being examples for others to see
For not following His law of sacrifices, for worshiping God
with disgrace and reluctancy

So Malachi warned them to repent of their sin so that God's
wrath might be turned away
For He should be feared among the nations, for He is truth
and truth He'll always convey
The men were also accused of marrying pagan women who
worshiped idols conscientiously
And of practicing divorce despised by God who always
demands commitment and sincerity

The people rejected the LORD'S holiness and justice,
challenging Him openly to intervene
So He announced the coming of the Messiah—a promise
for intercession—as a go-between
The LORD would come in judgment of sin; the priests
would be purged, properly purified
Sorcerers, adulterers, perjurers and oppressors of the poor
would be punished as prophesied

Again the LORD encouraged the people to return to Him,
but they denied they'd gone astray
Then they were charged with robbing God of tithes and
offerings, with failing to obey
So they spoke harshly against God, saying it didn't profit
them to surrender wholeheartedly
They ranted that the proud, the wicked and the tempters
prosper and escape without penalty

Men who were unfaithful to their wives started turning a
deaf ear to vows of holy wedlock
So God warned to heed marriage bonds He witnesses, for
commitment is no poppycock
Malachi foretold the day when the wicked and proud would
drive God to issue up desolation
Only the remnants, the faithful few, would be spared and
give God unspeakable elation

Read Malachi and recognize we must be willing and
faithful whenever we tithe
God is loving and patient, but has no tolerance for conceit,
no tolerance for our pride
Read Malachi and recognize we must regard marriage a
priority all of our born days
And must be willing to repent, willing to change our
wicked and sinful ways

Read Malachi and recognize God is faithful and true to the
promises by His hand
And our relationship is shattered whenever we disregard
His love and His command
Read Malachi and recognize our alienation from God is not
spent beyond repair
He can restore the withered heart and forgive by grace if we
cry out to Him in prayer

Read Malachi and recognize that those refusing to repent
will be judged and not blessed
So turn your life over to Him and make Him your beacon—
offer up your godly best

POEMS TO HONOR

THE NEW TESTAMENT

MATTHEW

"Where is He who has been born King of the Jews?
For we saw His star in the east
and have come to worship Him."
2:2

"Do not think that I came to abolish the Law or the
Prophets;
I did not come to abolish but to fulfill."
5:17

"Go therefore and make disciples of all the nations,
baptizing them in the name of the Father
and the Son and the Holy Spirit."
28:19

MATTHEW

A thousand years earlier, God had made an agreement with
David when he was king
Promising him a never-ending dynasty which his royal
bloodline would bring
Now that prophecy was in position, ready to be fulfilled—
to reach its highest expression
As the Messiah abided in the wings, all set to become King,
but not in earthly succession

Mary, a virgin, was with child through the Holy Spirit just
as Isaiah had prophesied
Fearing her disgrace, Joseph, her betrothed, planned to send
her to another town to reside
But an angel appeared to Joseph and revealed the truth
about Mary and her conception
Then Joseph obeyed and proceeded with plans to marry her,
which was God's direction

After Jesus was born in Bethlehem, the magi arrived in
Jerusalem from the east afar
And said they had come to worship the King of the Jews,
said they had seen His star
King Herod and all of Jerusalem were disturbed when the
magi inquired about the situation
So Herod planned to kill Jesus and tried to trick the magi
into revealing the infant's location

But after listening to Herod, they followed the star until it
stood over the baby's domicile
And rejoicing, they fell down and worshiped Him and
presented gifts to the Holy Child
Then in a dream they were warned by God not to return to
Herod as they had intended
So the magi left for their own country by another route as
the dream had recommended

When they had departed, Joseph had a dream revealing
Herod was searching for the Child
And was instructed to flee with his family to Egypt and
stay there till the Lord reconciled
Joseph obeyed and remained there until King Herod's
death—so prophecy would be fulfilled
Now when Herod realized the magi had tricked him, he
ordered certain male children killed

After Herod's death, an angel of the Lord advised Joseph to
take his family into Israel land
But when he arrived there, he heard that Judah's King
Archelaus was quite a violent man
Then after God warned Joseph of this fact, they journeyed
to a region of southern Galilee
And settled in a town called Nazareth which had been
marked long before in prophecy

John the Baptist preached in the wilderness as forerunner
for Jesus—his ministry, his chore
To prepare the way for Him as Isaiah had prophesied over
seven hundred years before
People from all around Judea and the Jordan flocked to
hear John's message to repent
Multitudes were baptized, set to hallow the name of the
coming Savior by being obedient

Then from Galilee to the Jordan River, Jesus came up to
John requesting to be baptized
But John thought Jesus—who had no sin—should baptize
him and felt unqualified
Still Jesus insisted it was fitting to fulfill all righteousness
and repeated His request
And when John baptized Him, the heavens opened up and
the trinity was manifest

Later in the wilderness, Jesus was tempted three times by
Satan and met him in confrontation
Testing His human side, He proved He would only obey the
Father, not worldly considerations
Satan couldn't persuade Him to trade God's Word for
passing glory by trying to manipulate
Couldn't persuade Jesus to worship him instead of God, the
only one worthy to elevate

When Jesus began His Galilean ministry, it was a measure
that fulfilled Isaiah's prophecy
That the Messiah would be a light to the land of Zebulun
and Naphtal, Gentiles of Galilee
Jesus began to preach John's very message, beseeching the
people of the urgency to repent
He called four fishermen—Peter, Andrew, James and
John—to follow Him with confidence

Preaching around Galilee, Jesus taught in synagogues—
here and there, around and about
He healed a great multitude and, from place to place,
crowds followed Him throughout
He warned His disciples about temptation, but assured them
of rewards in His Beatitudes
And at the Sermon on the Mount, He taught that believers
should be the light that exudes

Jesus taught God's Law and what the main point of the Law
really and truly should be
That obeying God's Law is more important than studying
or explaining it tenaciously
He taught about the danger of anger, and how the act of
lust—even the thought—is sin
That divorce cannot be used to disregard your vows, except
for unfaithfulness therein

Jesus taught about telling the truth, about not retaliating and
about loving your enemy
About giving without desiring praise, recognition or
reward, but with love and humility
He taught that the soul of prayer isn't public style, but for
God, private time you impart
And when praying, do not offer up shallow repetition, but
an honest and sincere heart

Jesus taught that we should not use fasting to get attention
from others with our holiness
But to go about normal daily routine and not set out to fish
for praise, trying to impress
And the motive for giving money toward God's work
should be only to obey His will
We can never serve both God and money, for God alone is
the one equipped to fulfill

In reference to criticizing, He calls us to judge not, but to
forgive and be discerning
Faults that bother us in others may be our own
shortcomings which our soul is churning
Jesus tells us not to worry about our needs, since God
promises us He will provide
Because worry can consume, disrupt, impact us and cause
our trust in God to subside

He wants us to be persistent in our efforts of pursuing
God—to ask, to seek, to knock
To treat people like you want them to treat you—the
Golden Rule intact, as our bedrock
The way to heaven is narrow, Jesus stipulated as He taught,
but it's the only path to eternity
The way to destruction is wide and inviting, and multitudes
pass through it frequently

Jesus warns to beware of those whose words sound holy,
but who are motivated by ego
With a hefty appetite for money, fame, power—exalting
self and minimizing Christ though
And they prophesy only what other people want to hear,
claiming it is God's Word
Identify them by their fruit and consistency in godly
action—by God's truth being heard

He exposes those who sound godly but have no relationship
with Him, the King of Kings
And says we must listen and obey as disciples and not be
phony or shallow in anything
For on that final day of reckoning, God will settle all, judge
sin and reward faith as well
So act on the Word, help others see that the results of
ignoring Him cannot be dispelled

Jesus performed many miracles—healing, driving out
demons, and calming a stormy sea
And gave His twelve disciples authority over unclean
spirits and healing of every variety
Jesus prepared His disciples to face persecution for
spreading the gospel with confidence
But following Him might cause separation from friends and
family, due to their obedience

In regard to Heaven, Jesus described it as a promised place
of rest for the weary soul
And declared an intimate relationship with the Father be
gained through the Son's control
Large crowds continued to follow Him around while
religious leaders strived to debase
But Jesus' discernment stopped their attempts to trick Him,
to deceive Him into disgrace

When speaking to crowds, Jesus used a plethora of parables
to help them understand
To help them grasp spiritual truth, encouraging them in
spiritual sowing as their plan
He also encountered people of His hometown of Nazareth
with their refusal to believe
And when Herod ordered John the Baptist beheaded, Jesus
withdrew in order to grieve

When Jesus asked His disciples about who people say He
is—He the Son of Man
Peter acknowledged Jesus as Christ, the divine—the Master
with the upper hand
Then Jesus predicted His death and resurrection to His
disciples, three times in all
But they didn't understand what all of that meant, couldn't
grasp the prophecy call

Jesus warned and duly condemned the religious leaders for
their downright hypocrisy
For they hungered mightily for more power, money,
status—slighting God thoroughly
Then on the Mount of Olive, Jesus taught His disciples
about the future days to come
Saying He would return, so be prepared while serving His
people to the maximum

Afterward, there was a deliberate plot to kill Jesus when
Passover had come to its close
And in exchange for thirty pieces of silver, Judas agreed to
betrayal—as the Scripture goes
At the Lord's Last Supper, Jesus declared that for one
disciple there was a dire prediction
And Judas dipped in the bowl with Him, sealing Him the
betrayer to initiate the crucifixion

Jesus predicted Peter's three denials after Peter had
declared he would never disown Him
And in His human flesh, Jesus agonized over His
approaching pain—pain more than grim
There in the Garden of Gethsemane, He fell on His face
and three times there He prayed
If it be His Father's will, He would rescue Him from the
price which lay ahead to be paid

Sometime later, Judas was accompanied by a large crowd,
swords and clubs in possession
After betraying Jesus with a kiss, the religious leaders
arrested Him without any discretion
The trial, held in haste before the high priest, was a
mockery of justice to the Messiah
And in the end, the Council decided He deserved death for
blasphemy—calling Him a liar

Then Peter denied knowing Jesus, as Jesus had predicted
when speaking with him before
And when Judas saw Jesus condemned, he felt terrible
remorse that cut clean to the core
Admitting his sin, he returned the thirty pieces of silver,
tossing it into the sanctuary
Then he departed from there and hanged himself, thus
fulfilling Scripture's prophecy

Jesus stood trial before Pontius Pilate and then He was
handed over to be crucified
Roman soldiers stripped Him and dressed Him in a scarlet
robe—woefully decried
They put a crown of thorns upon His head and placed a
reed in His right hand
They knelt down before Him and mocked Him for His
awesome faithful stand

They spat on Him, took the reed from His hand, and beat
mightily upon His head
Then afterwards, they took the robe away and put His
garments back on instead
They led Him away to be crucified with two thieves
positioned on either side
And from the sixth hour until the ninth, darkness fell upon
the land before He died

The veil of the temple was split in two and an earthquake
violently shook the ground
And those who had departed this life arose from the tombs
and appeared all around
When the centurions and guards who kept watch over Jesus
saw those miraculous events
"Truly this was the Son of God!" they said with fright,
witnessing significant incidents

Jesus was laid in the tomb and guards were posted to make
sure the grave was secure
For religious leader recalled Jesus saying that His
resurrection would occur for sure
But He conquered death anyhow, just as He had promised
He would do one day
Then told His disciples to go and make disciples of all
nations—to teach, to obey

As you read this Gospel, behold Jesus as Teacher, as
Master, as the King of Kings
Who was sent by the Father as our Messiah, our Lord and
Savior—to be our everything
He came to earth to die for us, to deliver us from ourselves,
from our rotten, wretched sin
To change lives, to prepare us for eternity—when our
earthly life meets its earthly end

MARK

"For even the Son of Man did not come to be served, but to serve, and to give His life a ransom for many."
10:45

MARK

Hundreds of years earlier, Isaiah had predicted John the
Baptist would announce the Messiah
Now John was spreading the news that Jesus' arrival was at
hand, like an anxious town crier
His message was coupled with baptism as a visible sign of
repentance for one's sins
And all of Judea went out to the Jordan to confess, to be
baptized and let new life begin

After being baptized by John, Jesus went into the
wilderness and was tempted by Satan there
For forty days He endured Satan's temptations as the angels
watched over Him with care
Then John was arrested and Jesus went to Galilee to preach
the gospel for everyone to heed
The long-awaited Messiah had come to urge all to repent;
His reign on earth had begun indeed

Later Jesus called four fishermen to come along and follow
Him, to become fishers of men
They were Simon, Andrew, James and John who left their
nets and went along with Him
Jesus taught in the synagogue with authority and drove out
an unclean spirit from a man
All were amazed and throughout Galilee the news spread,
the news of the Savior's hand

Preaching roundabout Galilee, Jesus healed a host of
people and cast out demons, too
He ate with Matthew, a tax collector, and with other sinners
who needed to start anew
And when Jesus told Matthew to follow Him, he arose and
obeyed the call that day
Then from Galilee and all around, great multitudes
followed Him all along the way

Out of scores of people who followed Him, Jesus chose
twelve with a heart to obey
And among the twelve were Peter who would deny Him
and Judas who would betray
These ordinary men would be taught by the Teacher until
molded into extraordinary men
He would send them out to preach and give them power to
heal and cast out demons then

The scribes accused Jesus of being under Satan's power,
attempting to destroy His popularity
But His response demonstrated that their argument carried
not one ounce of normalcy
Jesus taught by using parables to explain God's Word—to
compel people to think and comply
He calmed a raging sea and drove demons from a man into
a herd of swine feeding nearby

He raised the dead, restored sight, fed five thousand with
five loaves and two fish of the sea
He sent out His disciples in pairs to preach, to heal, and
cast out demons by His sovereignty
Then Herod, who feared and respected John the Baptist,
had him beheaded at his wife's request
Because he had offered his wife's daughter her desire, since
dancing pleased his dinner guests

The religious leaders, the Pharisees, who had tried to
explain away Jesus' great miracles before
Now came forward to test him, being argumentative, asking
for sign from above furthermore
But Jesus refused their demand and told them that no sign
would be given to that generation
Then leaving them, He put out to sea and sailed away to the
other side in utter exasperation

When Peter confessed Jesus as the Christ, Jesus warned His
disciples not to tell a living soul
He predicted His death and resurrection three times—to His
disciples these events were foretold
Taking Peter, James and John along with Him, Jesus was
transfigured up on a mountain high
He was exalted as the long-awaited Messiah and His divine
nature was revealed from the sky

Jesus warned against temptation and demonstrated that
discipline, though painful, is the price
In order to rid sin from our lives and become true followers,
you must experience sacrifice
Jesus taught about the sanctity of marriage and charged
commitment brings permanence
Saying God doesn't approve of divorce with the exception
of adultery set forth as evidence

Jesus taught that true greatness comes in serving others—
even for Him, the Son of Man
He did not come to be served, but to give His life a ransom
for many as God had planned
Then He rode into Jerusalem on a donkey as Zechariah had
predicted in times gone by
Later when He stood trial, the ones who'd shouted,
"Hosanna!" now shouted, "Crucify!"

Jesus exposed their real motives when the religious leaders
set out to challenge His authority
They tried to entrap Him, questioning Him about taxes, but
Jesus knew their hypocrisy
When they inquired about the resurrection, He proved
there's life after you pass away
And when asked which commandment was the greatest,
Jesus answered righteously that day

Jesus exposed religious leaders exploiting others while
pretending to be pious hypocritically
And taught that gifts of any size are pleasing to God if
given out of gratitude and generosity
His disciples asked Him about the future and Jesus revealed
much, warning them to beware
But most all, remember the things He had taught them and
remember to always be prepared

He told of His return and that no matter what happens,
God's Word will never pass away
And because no earthly soul knows when He'll return,
study and live God's Word each day
Be not misled by muddled allegations of thing to come or
speculate with your own expressions
Be not afraid to spread the gospel—stand by your faith and
face any persecution or oppression

The Jewish leaders were secretly plotting to seize Jesus
covertly and murder Him ultimately
Then in exchange for pieces of silver, Judas agreed to
betray Him when given the opportunity
The disciples prepared the Passover—the Lord's Last
Supper, still observed in worship today
And Jesus foretold that the one who dipped in the bowl
with Him was the one who'd betray

Jesus told His disciples they would scatter when He was
arrested as Zechariah had prophesied
That before the rooster crowed twice, Peter would deny
Him thrice—would deny the deified
Then Jesus was betrayed, arrested, questioned and three
times Peter denied knowing Him at all
The disciples deserted Him; the religious leader took Him
to Pilate to let him decide the call

The Roman soldiers mocked Him repeatedly and He was
led away to Golgotha to be crucified
They placed Him on the cross between two robbers, one on
His right and one on His left side
And there on the cross, He endured an agonizing and
tortuous death to save the world from sin
He was laid in a tomb, but arose from the dead to ensure a
chance for humanity to live again

After He arose, He appeared to Mary Magdalene and she
told His disciples as they grieved
But when they heard He was alive—that she had seen
Him—they utterly refused to believe
Then later He appeared to two believers on a road and to
the eleven disciples in reclination
And He instructed them to go into all the world, spreading
the gospel to all human creation

Read Mark and behold Jesus' true identity revealed not
only by His spoken words
But by His deeds as He served, as He sacrificed and saved
others undeterred
Read Mark and see Jesus' love and power—so mighty, so
steeped in deity
Be convinced that Jesus really is God who reaches out to
convict you and me

Read Mark and feel the pain of the piercing nails to save us
all from sin
Then open up your life to salvation and dare to let the Holy
Spirit move in

LUKE

And Jesus said to him,
"Today salvation has come to this house,
because he, too, is a son of Abraham.
For the Son of Man has come to seek
and to save that which was lost."
19:9-10

LUKE

In the days of Herod, Zacharias and Elizabeth were
obedient to God, living righteously
But had no children since Elizabeth was barren and both
were advanced in years considerably
Then an angel of the Lord appeared to Zacharias and
promised him a son they'd name John
Who'd prepare the way for the Messiah and turn many
from sin and to God they would respond

An angel promised the virgin, Mary, she would conceive
and bear the Son of the Omnipotent
And informed her of her aged and barren relative Elizabeth
who'd bear the son of Providence
After the angel explained, Mary agreed to carry the Child—
Jesus, whom God did choose
Then she hurried off to Judah to visit Elizabeth who was
filled with joy for her blessed news

John the Baptist, chosen by God, was born to be the
Messiah's forerunner—to pave the way
And Zacharias prophesied the coming of the Savior who
would redeem those gone astray
Then Jesus was born in Bethlehem and shepherds in the
field heeded the angel's sign
And headed straight to Bethlehem where they found the
holy child in a manger so divine

After eight days Jesus was taken to the temple to be
consecrated, keeping the law of the Lord
There the aged Simeon and Anna prophesied the Child's
future as God did so accord
The Child continued to grow in strength, to increase in
wisdom, and at twelve years of age
His parents took Him to Jerusalem to celebrate Passover,
where He'd take His debut stage

Returning from the Feast, they had traveled a day after
spending quite some time there
When His parents discovered Jesus had stayed behind, of
which they were unaware
They returned to Jerusalem and found Him in the temple
sitting amidst rabbis of the land
Attentive and popping questions, all marveled at the depth
to which He did understand

Now as was foretold, John the Baptist burst forth to prepare
the way for Jesus to begin
He preached repentance and baptizing, urging all to turn to
God for forgiveness of sin
Later John the Baptist would rebuke Herod for His sin of
living with Herodias immorally
She would treacherously plot his death, imprison him and
the worse would come to be

John the Baptist baptized Jesus in the river before the
tragedy of his circumstance occurred
And as Jesus was praying, the heavens opened up and the
Trinity converged in the Word
Then Satan tempted him in the wilderness, but He used
Scripture to resist attacks, to discern
And though Christ's defeat of Satan was decisive, Satan
would wait for a fitting time to return

Jesus began teaching throughout Galilee, but was rejected
in Nazareth where He was raised
He preached, taught, healed, raised the dead—performed
miracles with power truly displayed
Jesus had many disciples, but He selected only twelve
whom He'd endow with His authority
They were ordinary men He would groom—with different
backgrounds and personalities

Jesus presented the Beatitudes, describing what it means to
be a follower of Christ on earth
He used parables to communicate spiritual truth and to
motivate listeners to discover its worth
He empowered His disciples to have holy sanction over all
demons and heal diseases, too
He explained how to deal with tough times and held them
accountable for all they would do

Jesus predicted His death and resurrection three times, but
His disciples didn't comprehend
He laid out the cost for following Him—dedication, self-
denial and a discipline regimen
He sent out seventy-two messengers to prepare towns for
His visit—to minister one by one
When the seventy-two messengers returned, they were
joyful for victories already begun

Jesus taught His disciples how to communicate with God,
being persistent in prayer each day
To praise God, express needs, ask forgiveness, to forgive
any who wronged them in any way
Jesus spoke against hypocrisy—of appearing to respect
God when the heart is separated
And called the people to repent of their sins or they would
perish in kind if they deviated

When He rode into Jerusalem on a donkey, the whole
crowd sang praises to God joyfully
But the Pharisees asked Jesus to silence them, for they
hated any challenge of their authority
Jesus let them know that if the people were quieted, discord
would ensue in demonstrations
He wept over the city, prophesying that suffering would gag
Jerusalem for refusing salvation

Religious leaders questioned Jesus about paying taxes and
about whether there is resurrection
Jesus responded with questions they could not answer,
warning to beware of misdirection
He prepared His disciples for tough days ahead and
cautioned that false Messiahs would come
But assured them He would return and salvation would
spread, so let God's will be done

Because they feared Jesus' followers, the chief priest and
scribes sought to kill Him secretly
Then Satan entered Judas and he informed the leaders of a
way to betray Jesus for the enemy
They were happy for Judas' offer to turn traitor and agreed
to pay him for being the deceiver
Judas consented and endeavored to pursue an opportunity
for betrayal for those unbelievers

At the Passover, Jesus predicted Judas would betray Him
and thrice Peter would deny
With His disciples, He went up to the Mount of Olives and
anguished over His plight to die
Then as foretold, Jesus was betrayed when Judas
approached to kiss Him—a sign of treachery
Then Peter denied knowing Jesus three times and, recalling
the Lord's prediction, wept bitterly

The religious leaders quickly condemned Him, but Pilate
found Him innocent of the accusations
He sent Him to Herod's domain, but Herod sent Him back
to Pilate after mockery and imitations
Again Pilate found no guilt in Him and three times said he
would punish and release Him then
But the crowd kept insisting He be crucified and Pilate
turned Him over to the fixated men

They led Him away and Simon of Cyrene was seized to
carry the cross for Jesus that day
Large crowds followed Him to His death and women
mourned as He passed along the way
There at the place called The Skull, along with two
common criminals hanging on either side
Jesus asked God to forgive His accusers for their ignorance
of the Light as He was crucified

Jesus committed His Spirit to the heavenly Father and
breathed His very last breath
And when the centurion saw all that had happened, he
praised God after Jesus' death
"Certainly this man was innocent," he said, expressing his
heart in holy revelation
For He must have realized this event carried phenomenal
and spiritual implications

Joseph of Arimathea asked for the body, secured it and laid
Him in the tomb with care
And on the third day at early dawn, some women came
with spices they had prepared
But they discovered the tomb was empty and saw the stone
had been rolled away
And two men suddenly stood near in dazzling clothes,
terrifying the women that day

The two revealed Jesus had risen and reminded them of the
words of His prediction
That He'd be delivered to sinful men, crucified and arise
the third day after His crucifixion
The women remembered, telling the disciples what they'd
seen—the resurrection phase
The disciples disbelieved them, but Peter ran to examine
the tomb and was so amazed

As two believers were walking along the road, talking
about the event that had taken place
Jesus appeared and walked along with them, but they were
curbed from recognizing His face
In awe, they continued discussing history's greatest event;
but were in doubt, didn't believe
After they express their sadness and confusion, Jesus used
Scripture to help them perceive

Approaching their destination, it was getting late so they
urged Jesus to stay with them
And it wasn't until Jesus broke the bread and blessed it did
they recognized Him
But then Jesus vanished from sight and they retraced the
day's journey and their hearts
And immediately arose and hurried to His disciples and
their experience they did impart

While they were imparting those experiences, Jesus
appeared and said, "Peace be to you"
All were startled and seized with fright, thinking it was a
ghost standing within their view
Only when He pointed out nail marks on His hands and feet
did they begin to understand
And to assure them it was really Jesus Himself, He ate
some fish like any mortal man

Jesus appeared to His disciples again, opening their minds
to grasp the Scripture's prophecies
Which foretold He'd suffer and rise the third day as
fulfillment of God's Word perfectly
And said repentance and forgiveness of sin would be
proclaimed to all nations in His name
That His disciples must go and spread the good news after
the Holy Spirit at Pentecost came

Jesus took His disciples as far as Bethany and then lifted up
His hands and blessed them
And while He was offering blessings, He was taken up to
heaven and they all worshiped Him
Then with great joy, they returned to Jerusalem and spent
much time blessing God with praise
Redemption had been accomplished and now all could look
to Jesus and emulate His ways

Read Luke and observe Christ's life without blemish, with
the offer of salvation
He forgives those who accept Him as Lord of their lives, as
Lord of all creation
You must believe what He says is perfection and truth—
every single word
That Jesus is God who loves us to pieces—His promise will
not be deferred

Read Luke and find the Holy Spirit as God's confirmation
of Jesus' authority
Read Luke and hear Christ's call to forsake all and follow
Him unconditionally

JOHN

"For God so loved the world,
that He gave His only begotten Son,
that whoever believes in Him
shall not perish, but have eternal life."
3:16

Many other signs Jesus also performed
in the presence of the disciples,
which are not written in this book;
but these have been written so that you may believe
that Jesus is the Christ, the Son of God;
and that believing you may have life in His name.
20:30-31

JOHN

Jesus—completely human and completely God—always
existed, never ceased to be
He lights the path for folks to find their way and teaches
them to walk faithfully
Even though He created the world, His very own riddled
Him with fierce rejection
But those who received Him became God's own with their
surrender and His direction

The Pharisees sent priests and Levites to inspect John the
Baptist's foreseen mission
They asked if he was the Christ, Elijah or the prophet—
they asked with much suspicion
John confessed he was neither, that preparing the way for
the Messiah was his holy election
That he baptized in water, but there was one they hadn't
met, of pure and holy perfection

The next day Jesus came to be baptized and after the
baptism John the Baptist realized
Jesus was the Messiah who came to indwell believers with
the Holy Spirit—all who complied
Then John pointed two of his disciples to Jesus and those
two followed Him immediately
Afterward, others came as Jesus' disciples and followed
eagerly with thirst and loyalty

Alongside His mother and disciples in Cana at Galilee, He
turned water into wine there
And when money changers and traders used the temple for
greed—a money-making affair
Jesus was outraged at their exploitation of others—at
making the house of God a mockery
So He chased them out, overturning tables, and tossed their
coins away with authority

When Nicodemus was searching and believed Jesus
possessed the answers he needed
He visited Jesus by night to be taught truth and to test Jesus
himself unimpeded
Jesus explained the significance of a spiritual rebirth and
how in Him you must believe
About the Light and darkness, about fear of exposing self,
and how eternal life is received

John the Baptist was still preaching about repentance and
was baptizing converts dutifully
But his disciples were uneasy since people were following
Jesus instead of his ministry
Then John reminded them he was not Christ; that he was
sent to prepare the Messiah's way
That he was not the one, but was merely trying to direct
folks to Jesus—this he did convey

When Jesus heard controversy about baptizing more
believers than John being expressed
He left Judea for Galilee and along the way He stopped off
in Samaria in order to rest
He met a Samaritan woman by a well and ardently shared
the gospel with her there
Then the woman went into the city to share her experience,
to make others aware

In Galilee the people had already seen all the things He had
done at Jerusalem's feast
He was received warmly and healed an official's son there
who had nearly deceased
Then He healed a lame man in Jerusalem who for thirty-
eight years had been lying ill
Since it was the Sabbath, He was accused of blasphemy and
was sought out to be killed

Jesus claimed to be the Son of God who is equal to God,
who offer eternal life to mankind
He claimed to be the source of life—the Creator who
judges sin, who is truly divine
His claims were supported by John the Baptist who
testified that what He spoke was true
Because the Old Testament points to the Messiah,
mentioning Moses' prophecy, too

At Tiberias Jesus fed five thousand miraculously and
walked on water in the Sea
The next day He explained why He is the bread of life and
how believers gain eternity
The Jews disagreed that He was from Heaven and didn't
believe the message they heard
When He taught in the synagogue in Capernaum, the
Jewish leaders rejected His Word

Therefore many disciples pivoted and deserted Him,
wouldn't walk with Him anymore
And Jesus asked His twelve if they wished to withdraw, but
they stood as firm as before
Then Jesus revealed that, in spite of them being His choice,
one of them was evil though
Of course, Judas Iscariot was the one He meant—the one
who'd betray Him as we know

The Pharisees still sought to kill Him and at first his own
brothers doubted what He'd say
And they ridiculed Him about His ability to really work
miracles, all in a sarcastic way
He openly taught in the temple, but considerable grumbling
erupted among the multitude
All the talk was about Jesus, yet no one supported Him, not
one had the courage to intrude

Some believed, some were hostile, some disqualified Jesus
as the Messiah who had come
The Pharisees resisted the truth and wanted to seize Him,
saying He wasn't the chosen one
Yet the officers didn't arrest Him, reporting that never had a
man spoken the way He spoke
And Nicodemus questioned their failure to keep their own
laws—their logic he revoked

While Jesus taught in the temple, the Jewish leaders used a
woman in an adulterous condition
To test Him and trick Him, they recalled Moses' stoning
law; then asked Jesus His position
Jesus replied that only a sinless person would throw the
first stone, upholding legal judgment
After the leaders quietly slipped away, Jesus forgave the
woman and advised her to repent

Still teaching in the temple, Jesus declared He was the
Light of the world—the chosen one
But there within the treasury, no one apprehended Him
because His hour had not yet come
He warned of judgment to come and spoke of God's
children, those who believe and obey
And when He said He existed before Abraham, they tried to
stone Him, but He slipped away

After Jesus healed the man blind from birth, the Pharisees
questioned the man repeatedly
The man was reviled and evicted from the synagogue, but
Jesus found him and the Pharisees
The man had found new life in Christ and learned the depth
of spiritual blindness that day
Jesus explained to the Pharisees how sin blinded them, how
complacency allowed it to stay

Jesus taught that He is the door, our access to God—the
good shepherd of hope and purity
Again some discredited Him while others believed He was
God just as He claimed to be
The Jews were ready to stone Him, but He rebuked them
with Scripture, the ultimate evidence
They tried seizing Him again, but He eluded them and
found believers of His Omnipotence

In Bethany, Mary and Martha sent word to Jesus that
Lazarus was as sick as could be
Though Jesus was their friend, when He heard the new, He
didn't respond immediately
So Lazarus died and when Jesus arrived, He wept and then
raised him from the dead
When the Jewish leaders heard this, they convened to plot
His death, but again Jesus fled

Mary anointed Jesus' feet with very costly perfume and
wiped His feet with her hair
And Judas questioned why the perfume wasn't sold to
secure money for the poor to share
But Jesus implored him to leave Mary alone so she might
save it for His burial day details
And still crowds stopped by to see the miracle of Lazarus
and his death was planned as well

Jesus rode into Jerusalem on a donkey and the large crowd
that attended the celebration
Took branches of palm trees and shouted, "Hosanna!" and
welcomed Him with exaltation
They praised God, thinking Jesus was to be their king
who'd return it to its former glory
They were blind to His real mission, foretold by the
prophets, written in Scripture's stories

Then at the feast Jesus enlightened the listeners, explaining
why He must pay the price
But despite the proof He offered, most of them would not
believe He was the sacrifice
That He came to be the Light of the world, to rescue from
darkness all who'd believe
That He did not come to judge, but came to show how
salvation can surely be achieved

Jesus washed his disciples' feet to show they must serve
God, each other and humanity
Then at the Last Supper, He predicted Judas would betray
Him—and betrayal is disloyalty
When Peter spoke to Jesus, saying He'd lay down his life
for Him—to that he testified
Jesus foretold before the rooster crowed, Peter would deny
Him thrice as prophesied

Jesus promised His disciples the Holy Spirit would help
them recall all He'd taught before
He used the vine and the branches to teach about God, true
believers and false ones who ignore
He taught them about hatred in the world and noted that
toward Him many harbored hostility
He taught that after His glorification, believers could—in
Jesus' name—talk with God directly

Jesus prayed for His disciples and for those yet to come
who would believe God's Word
He prayed that His disciples would stand as unified
witnesses so that truth would be heard
He prayed that the world might know that God sent Him,
the one whose love prevails true
He prayed that love would indwell His people, a love that
refines and makes you brand new

Leading the temple guard to Jesus, Judas betrayed Him in
front of His disciples' eyes
And there they arrested Him, bound Him and delivered
Him to the high priest to be tried
Peter denied knowing Jesus as He was being questioned
and abused, as it all accumulated
Pilate found Him innocent, yet the Jews pleaded, with no
authority to order Him eliminated

Then Pilate tried to give that responsibility to someone else
since he was lacking evidence
And he tried to find a way of evading the issue, to release
Jesus who had proved His innocence
He tried to compromise by having Jesus soundly whipped
rather than turning Him over to die
And tried appealing to the sympathy of His accusers, but
the only cry alive was "Crucify!"

So Pilate handed Him over to them and Jesus was led away
bearing His cross that day
And there at Golgotha—two thieves on either side—they
crucified Him and He passed away
His body was bound and laid in a tomb nearby, but He
arose from the dead as prophesied
And appeared to Mary Magdalene and His disciples, and
Thomas and Peter were edified

Read the Gospel of John and discover the revelation of
Jesus' true identity
The Son of God, the Light of the world accurately
accentuate His deity
Read the Gospel of John and discover Jesus revealed in His
death and resurrection
Then accept the invitation to give your life to Him in a
joyful, holy connection

Read John and believe!
Read John and breathe!

ACTS

"But you will receive power
when the Holy Spirit has come upon you;
and you shall be My witnesses both in Jerusalem,
and in all Judea and Samaria,
and even to the remotest part of the earth."
1:8

ACTS

Following Jesus' death, His disciples scattered, were
disillusioned and afraid during that phase
After His resurrection, He appeared to His disciples and
taught them over a period of forty days
They became convinced that Jesus did arise and learned
about God's kingdom and its worth
And by believing in Him, they would soon receive the Holy
Spirit—their power source on earth

Jesus promised them that after they received the Holy
Spirit, Christ's power beyond compare
Then they would be able to witness in Jerusalem, in all of
Judea, in Samaria and everywhere
Afterward, while the disciples watched, Jesus was lifted up
into a cloud and out of sight
And two angels appeared, explaining that He would return
the same way in heavenly delight

The eleven returned to Jerusalem and proceeded to the
upper room in which they stayed
And along with Jesus' family—all one mind—they
expressed their devotion as they prayed
Later, Peter announced Judas' death which fulfilled the
Scripture long ago foretold
So between two men, they drew lots for his replacement
and Matthias entered the fold

When the day of Pentecost arrived, the disciples were all
gathered together in one location
When suddenly they were filled with the Holy Spirit and
spoke in tongues in manifestation
Then Peter stirred the crowd and told them why they should
listen and truly take heed
For the prophecies had been completed and Jesus could
forever change their lives indeed

In his sermon, Peter beseeched them to repent and turn to
Christ for forgiveness of their sin
About three thousand souls were saved that day as the Holy
Spirit came to reside within
Then instead of a lame beggar receiving his request for
money, Peter healed the man
He leaped and began walking and praising God, with the
people in awe of God's hand

With the people full of amazement, Peter used that unique
moment as a grand opportunity
To share Christ—how He was rejected, yet died for our sin,
how He could change their reality
As the gospel was shared, the Sadducees and others
grabbed Peter and John, arresting both men
But later released them, commanding them not ever to
speak or teach in Jesus' name again

Peter and John returned to the other disciples and reported
the threat and its implication
Then lifted their voices and prayed to God, asking for His
help to deal with the situation
They asked that they would continue spreading the gospel
with boldness and confidence
That in Jesus' name they'd carry on healing and rendering
miracles in faithful obedience

The congregation of believers was of one heart and soul—
all willing to give and share
So poverty among them was eliminated—not one suffered
while others had plenty to spare
But Ananias and Sapphira lied to God and His people when
they sold a piece of property
They said they gave more than they'd given and God's
judgment wrought death for fibbery

People from all around Jerusalem were gathering, bringing
those wishing to be healed
This filled the high priest with jealousy, so they arrested the
apostles who refused to yield
But during the night an angel of the Lord opened the prison
gates, releasing them instantly
The officers found them teaching in the temple and they
were arrested again with no brutality

Then Peter and the apostles declared to the council that
they must obey God rather than men
And when the council heard this, they were extremely
furious and intended to get rid them
But a Pharisee named Gamaliel advised them to stay away
from the apostles, to let the men be
They concurred but flogged them, ordering them not to
preach the gospel and set them free

As the disciples increased, an internal problem in the
church developed which was expressed
Greek-speaking Christians complained that their widows
weren't getting food like the rest
To correct this unfair treatment, the apostles chose seven
godly men of good reputation
And put those in charge who would devote themselves to
prayer and point others to salvation

Stephen was one of the seven, performing great wonders
and signs—full of power and grace
But some men couldn't cope with the wisdom and spirit
with which he spoke in that place
The angry Jewish leaders were intolerant of his words and
miracles, so they dragged him away
The council heard his plea, but they drove him out of the
city and stoned him to death that day

That set off great persecution of the church in Jerusalem as
believers scattered here and there
And Saul began ravaging Christian homes, dragging them
to prison without thought or care
The scattered and persecuted continued spreading the
gospel as Jesus had commanded they do
Like Philip who met a Scripture-reading Ethiopian, led him
to Christ, and baptized him, too

Now Saul, who still regularly persecuted Christians, was
traveling to Damascus one day
While on the road, there flashed a light and he fell to the
ground and heard a voice say
"Saul, Saul, why are you persecuting Me?" Then Jesus told
Saul what his course would be
When Saul arose, his fellow travelers led him straight to
Damascus because he could not see

He was blinded for a period of three days and consumed
neither food nor drink, but then
Through a vision, the Lord commanded Ananias to lay
hands on Saul so he might see again
And filled with the Holy Spirit, he was baptized, took food
and was strengthened subsequently
After several days among believers, he began proclaiming
Christ prior to his global ministry

Those who heard him knew he had previously persecuted
Christians for their righteousness
But Saul continued in his new life, refuting the Jewish
view, with evidence he possessed
Then the Jews plotted to dispose of him, but his disciples
assisted him in escaping by night
In Jerusalem, with his reputation, Christians feared him—
didn't believe he'd seen the light

As Peter traveled throughout the regions, he healed and
raised the dead in a steady affair
Then in a vision, Cornelius a godly man was told to send
men to Joppa to find Peter there
Peter too had a vision, advising that no longer should
Gentiles be treated with inferiority
Cornelius' men brought Peter to him and then Cornelius
and others were saved blessedly

The apostles and the brethren throughout Judea heard the
news of Gentiles accepting salvation
So when Peter came to Jerusalem, the Jews took issue with
his witnessing, with no trepidation
But Peter explained all that had happened to him and
Cornelius, in God's visions of Gentiles
And once they had heard Peter's story, they bit their
tongues and praised their God awhile

Afterward, there were those disciples who continued to
spread the gospel to Jews alone
But those who spoke the Word to Gentiles saw many
believe and become the Lord's own
Then for a year at the church in Antioch, Barnabas and Saul
taught those who believed
And there the disciples were first called Christians and the
first church was conceived

Then when Peter was arrested and imprisoned, the church
prayed for his release fervently
And an angel of the Lord appeared and awakened him,
unchained his hands and set him free
Peter followed the angel to the house of Mary, mother of
John, where many were in prayer
And when they opened the door and saw him, they were
amazed at beholding him there

Antioch held prophets and teachers, but the Holy Spirit set
Barnabas and Saul apart that day
There was work they were called to do, so everyone fasted,
prayed and sent them on their way
They began their missionary journey traveling all around,
proclaiming God's holy Word
Once Saul, known now as Paul, confronted a false prophet
until he believed the truth he heard

Paul's second missionary journey, along with Silas,
included many cities of his first ministry
In Lystra, he met a young Greek, Timothy, whom he
circumcised and mentored dutifully
As the churches continued to strengthen in faith and
number, Lydia was converted in Philippi
She, the very first convert in Europe, was baptized so she in
Christ could truly identify

There was a fortune-telling slave girl who was being
exploited by her masters monetarily
Paul cast out an evil spirit and her masters seized Paul and
Silas and took them to the authorities
The chief magistrates beat them with rods, threw them in
prison and fastened their feet in stocks
But after they prayed to God, an earthquake occurred and
the doors and chains unlocked

When the jailer awoke and thought the two had escaped, he
drew his sword to commit suicide
But Paul cried out to let him know they were still there and
he was converted—his life solidified
Eventually Paul and Silas were released and traveled to
Thessalonica to a synagogue of the Jews
They shared the gospel and many Greeks turned, including
women, once hearing the good news

But the jealous Jews attacked Jason's house where they
thought both were hidden out of sight
Then the authorities received a pledge from Jason and they
were released and sent away by night
When they arrived in Berea, the people there received the
Word with eagerness and glee
But Thessalonian Jews came to Berea to incite the crowd,
so Paul was ejected immediately

Paul and his companions, spread the gospel from Athens to
Corinth; then to Antioch he returned
After spending some time there, he departed and began the
third leg of his missionary sojourn
As he traveled spreading the gospel, there were setbacks
and victories as believers steadily increased
Once he drove an evil spirit from a man in Ephesus and
many occultists confessed and ceased

A riot in Ephesus caused Paul to head for Macedonia and
then off to Greece he proceeded
As he set sail for Syria, a plot against his life was devised,
so he backtracked unimpeded
Still faced with many adversities throughout the journey
and against advice of his friends
He headed to Jerusalem because it was God's will—a good
and faithful servant until the end

In time Paul arrived in Jerusalem where he was seized,
beaten and bound with chains, but still
Paul used this time of persecution as an opportunity to
defend the faith as he delivered his appeal
The next day he was unchained and brought before the
council to stand trial for some accusation
But a conspiracy to kill Paul persisted, so he was moved by
night to Caesarea for his preservation

Later, Paul eloquently presented his appeal before three
leaders in succession—as a captive, too
Then, when sent to Rome by sea, he was shipwrecked, but
his God brought him safely through
Finally in Rome—under house arrest—Paul delivered his
appeal, spreading the gospel even more
As he persevered, God's Word spread as Christianity
exploded, opening its holy heavenly door

Read Acts and experience the Holy Spirit doing a work in
the lives of ordinary men
Spreading the gospel and, like Paul, establishing the
Christian church for time without end
Read Acts and experience heroes and martyrs, miracles and
witnessing—birthing Christianity
And you'll see the possibility of someone like you
changing the world and Christian history

Read Acts and imagine bringing a brother to Christ—
imagine the joy, imagine the thrill
Read Acts and decide to commit yourself to witness by
faith and satisfy God's divine will

ROMANS

Therefore, having been justified by faith,
we have peace with God through our Lord Jesus Christ.
5:1

And do not be conformed to this world,
but be transformed by the renewing of your mind,
so that you may prove what the will of God is,
that which is good and acceptable and perfect.
12:2

ROMANS

Paul wrote to the Romans from Corinth and began by
humbling himself as a servant of Christ
Recounting the gospel to them, he manifested teachings of
the Scripture, the truth so precise
He expressed his and God's love, and his gratitude and
prayers for them became known
Then he declared his allegiance to the gospel, saying
righteousness comes by faith alone

Paul explained how people reject God, devise ideas of a
god and woo sin with sheer delight
He continued, maintaining that you can't be righteous by
your own strength in God's sight
For humanity is lost, wallowing in sin, with a need for
God's mercy and exoneration
So to avoid punishment and live forever with Christ
depends on God's grace for salvation

Paul informed the Roman believers that all are
unacceptable before God, all are condemned
But through Christ, we can stand before Him, justified by
faith—our lives made whole in Him
So we can feel the welcome freedom of a new life when
we're no longer under sin's scourge
Whereby we needn't serve by obeying law, but out of love
for God with renewed hearts purged

In this letter, Paul described the freedom from sin which
comes from being saved by grace
How it makes you feel to live for Christ and witness God's
love in His utmost embrace
He expressed his concern for his Jewish brethren and how
they clearly fit into God's plan
How God provided a way for both Jews and Gentiles to be
saved by faith, by the Son of Man

Paul said we must submit our lives completely to Christ in
a holy and sacrificial way
Use spiritual gifts of prophecy, service, exhortation, giving,
leadership, or mercy on display
Also, we must genuinely love others, be good citizens, but
follow the Lamb of God fervently
Monitor the effect your behavior has on others, building
each other up in faith and dignity

He emphasized unity among Christians—Christ's love
sprinkled among Jews and Gentiles
In conclusion, Paul reiterated his reason for writing to the
Romans over ever so many miles
Then he greeted his friends—Jews and Gentiles all,
prisoners and prominent citizens, too
And exclaimed the wonder of how prophecy of saving
Gentiles worldwide really came true

Read Romans and know that sin causes us to live our own way
It cuts us off from our God when we rebel, when we
disobey
Read Romans and know that we cannot remove sin, cannot
earn salvation
Due to Christ's death—the penalty for our sin—we can
defeat temptation

Read Romans and know that once we are saved, we are
sanctified
We are set apart from sin to grow, with Christ inside as our
holy guide
Read Romans and know no can be Christ-like alone, none
without unity
To fully express Christ, the entire body of Christians must
serve in symphony

1 CORINTHIANS

I do all things for the sake of the gospel,
so that I may become a fellow partaker of it.
9:23

1 CORINTHIANS

Paul had heard reports that there were quarrels among the
Corinthians in that community
So he wrote to them to address the problem and confusion,
and to squash out degeneracy
He stressed the message of the gospel and the role of the
church leaders was explained
Then he insisted that they grow in faith and live God's
Word righteously unrestrained

Immorality of certain members needed to be dealt with and
Paul noted this depravation
Such as the man having an affair with his father's wife, as
the church ignored the situation
The Corinthian believers refused to discipline them, to
settle their own affairs internally
So Paul condemned sexual sin, making it clear Christians
don't partake in such immorality

Previously, the Corinthians had written to Paul with
questions relating to problems within
So in the remainder of the letter, he responded to them so
they'd understand holy discipline
Due to the spread of prostitution and infidelity, marriages
were in ruins—in total disarray
So Paul advised that Christians can't blend in with society's
values, but only live God's way

Concerning eating meat sacrificed to idols, it may be
perfectly okay, Paul pointedly said
But if anything causes others to stumble, refrain from
taking liberty for their good instead
Speaking of worship, Paul explained the Christian role of
everyone—worship's disposition
He valued observing the Lord's Supper and said spiritual
gifts must boost spiritual conditions

But love is more important than all the other spiritual gifts
in the Church, he did contend
Without love, other gifts yield little since love creates
godliness which spontaneously blends
Paul concluded with a discourse on the certainty, order and
mystery of Christ's resurrection
Then offered practical values for Christians, ending with
divine blessings and holy affection

Read 1 Corinthians and realize we shouldn't ignore
problems in the church or in our lives
Instead, confront any specific Christian and deal with
situations head-on as they arise
Read 1 Corinthians and realize that love and unity in a
church portray true Christianity
And they are more important in the Master's plan than
leaders and labels could ever be

Read 1 Corinthians and realize Christians mustn't follow
society and accept its lifestyle
Rather, live Christ-like, pleasing to God's eye—lives holy,
loving, and worthwhile

2 CORINTHIANS

Therefore, if anyone is in Christ, he is a new creature;
the old things passed away;
behold, new things have come.
5:17

Test yourselves to see if you are in the faith;
examine yourselves!
Or do you not recognize this about yourselves,
that Jesus Christ is in you—
unless indeed you fail the test?

2 CORINTHIANS

Paul was concerned about false teachers who backstabbed
him and refuted authority
So he wrote the Corinthians to defend his position, to
denounce twisting truth invariably
He explained the essence of a Christian ministry and taught
them to discern and choose
So here's more significant advice He offered them to use
when spreading the good news:

Beware of false teachers claiming to be effective and
honorable without God—how absurd!
They boast of their own power and prestige, thinking
they're adequate without God's Word
Saying you're saved by merely keeping the old law results
in death—no grace or mercy be
But under the new covenant, if you believe in Christ, you
receive new life and gain eternity

When spreading the gospel, you're in the presence of God
and He hears every word you say
Take heed not to distort the message to please the audience,
but herald God's truth His way
Although some affliction may cause you to think it's
hopeless, you haven't reached the end
Through all your sins and suffering, God never abandons
you—He's your greatest friend

The bodies we live in now are only temporal; the flesh is
not all your life will ultimately be
For there is life after death whereby we'll live with God
forever—no pain, no sin in eternity
So don't be so wrapped up in worldly prosperity that
defiles the mind, that's not of the heart
And avoid false teachers more concerned with self than
Christ; avoid the words they impart

Believers, be vigorous in witnessing to the lost for Christ,
but one thing you mustn't try
Don't link up with them in personal or business
relationships; here's the reason why:
Such association could cause you to compromise the faith,
could put you in great jeopardy
So do everything possible to avoid situations that might
compel you to divide your loyalties

If you are sorry for wrongdoings just because you were
caught or for other results of your sin
That is "sorrow of the world" and doesn't lead to a changed
heart, but to death in the end
Now repentance according to the will of God leads to
changed behavior, leads to true salvation
For when you renounce your sin, you reclaim your faith
and accept correction and restoration

It's not the amount of the gift you give to God; it's your
heart condition instead—here's why
If you give with a grudging heart, you don't please Him and
His blessings will pass you by
Give cheerfully out of your devotion to Christ, out of love
for those who are believers like you
Give cheerfully out of joy of helping the needy, give
because it's simply the right thing to do

Don't compare yourself to someone else; pride makes you
feel you're better than another
Measure yourself against God's principles and don't
compare to another sister or brother
You shouldn't worry about others' success or want
recognition for something you did well
Just let your life be Christ-like; seek God's praise—not
man's whose truth can't be upheld

Don't be fooled by external appearances, by Bible-quoting
leaders who mislead and deceive
Don't follow them into cults that alienate you from your
family and lead you to falsely believe
They're smooth-talking and appear good and moral, but
will lead you into evil and immorality
So don't let impressions alone guide you; scrutinize them
to see if they're Christians honestly

Do their teachings confirm the Scriptures, assuring the
certainty, the validity of God's Word?
Do they firmly declare and proclaim the truth that Jesus
Christ is God as written once it's heard?
Do they believe Jesus came to earth as a man to bring
salvation, to save you from sin that be?
And do their life-styles conform to standards consistent
with Biblical standards and morality?

When confronted with any affliction, such as the thorn in
Paul's flesh which caused debilitation
Let it remind you of your constant need for God and
humble you to always seek his inspiration
To rely on Him for your strength rather than on your own
effort, your understanding and energy
Let your weakness help develop your character and deepen
your worship with Him earnestly

Read 2 Corinthians and see if you are a Christian, if you
can pass the test
Is Christ's presence and power in your life real and is it
being manifest?
Read 2 Corinthians and see if you apply His standards even
in difficulties
And if love moves you to confront others with compassion
and with honesty

GALATIANS

It is for freedom that Christ has set us free.
Stand firm, then,
and do not let yourselves be burdened again
by a yoke of slavery.
5:1

GALATIANS

Some Jewish teachers in the churches of Galatia were
spreading false information
They insisted that Gentiles must obey Jewish traditions
along with their salvation
That faith in Christ wasn't enough, distorting the gospel to
cripple the joy of good news
So Paul wrote to the churches to refute that lie, to call
believers back to godly views

He told how he had once persecuted Christians and how
God changed his heart one day
How after conversion, he spent years preparing for ministry
which God called him to obey
And before sharing with the Gentiles, he let church leaders
know the message he'd exhale
So they'd understand, approve or disapprove, to prevent
controversy in the church as well

Paul related how he resisted religious leaders with no
allegiance to Christ, none to His glory
How he wasn't intimidated by the high and powerful, for all
are equal in the Father's story
Paul was entrusted with the gospel to reach Gentiles and
God used Peter to reach the Jews
He worked in the hearts of both men to effectively bring all
people the glorious good news

Peter, a church leader, was afraid of what other Jewish
Christians might think he embraced
So when he came to Antioch, Paul confronted him and
others, opposing them face-to-face
He told them the law can never make us acceptable to
God—by works man isn't justified
But only by faith in Christ will we discover the path to
salvation and with Him be crucified

Paul reminded the Galatians that when they believe, they
receive the Holy Spirit within
That obeying the law doesn't draw them to God—God's
spirit changes not like the wind
The law teaches the need for salvation, but God's grace
offers it—by faith submissively
So live up to faith in Christ, not to demands of others
who'll steal your joy and humility

Paul continued by saying Christ died to free us from sin so
we're not subject to slavery's call
So if in keeping the law, you are trying to save yourself,
you will encounter a mighty fall
Trying to *only* keep God's law separates you from God—
your deeds of service aren't enough
If rejected for standing for Christ, remember they rejected
Him too—so stand tall and tough

Paul kept up his confrontation, saying we are called to
freedom, but not to freedom to sin
So don't turn your freedom into "an opportunity for the
flesh," for Satan to wilily creep in
But through love, serve one another because you're free to
glorify God and do what is right
When we aren't moved by love, we are open to seeing fault
rather than strength and light

To Christians: Never depend on self and do not feel you are
exempt from helping another
Bear each other's burdens, working together for the good of
all—for each sister and brother
Do not compare yourself to others; let Christ be the model
that inspires you to your best
Bear your own loads; if you don't measure up, Christ will
love and accept you nevertheless

In closing, Paul reminds us that man's rules and taboos
aren't the measure of faith at all
But it is grace and faith, the truth of the gospel, freeing us
in Christ with His urgent call
The only way to foil worldly influences is to run to Him
with a thirst for the Word crucified
With your concern for finding salvation all wrapped up
with the condition of the heart inside

Read Galatians and find freedom in Christ Jesus through
Calvary
Find freedom from the bondage of sin, find freedom from
slavery
And don't allow legalism and sin to enslave you in Satan's
dreadful cell
Just use your freedom to live for Christ—His grace a story
to tell

Read Galatians and see
In Christ, you're free!

EPHESIANS

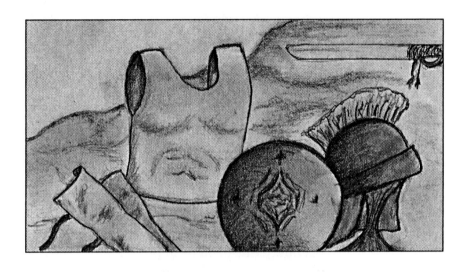

One Lord, one faith, one baptism,
one God and Father of all who is over all
and through all and in all.
4:5-6

Put on the full armor of God,
so that you will be able to stand firm
against the schemes of the devil.
6:11

EPHESIANS

Wanting to strengthen the believers in Ephesus in their faith
with much encouragement
Paul wrote to the Ephesians to explain the nature and
purpose of the church, its holy intent
To offer deep teaching on exactly how to nurture the church
and how to maintain its unity
And to remind them they must possess God's love, so
here's Paul's advice to God's family:

Through Christ, God's purpose is to save all, to unite Jew
and Gentile through salvation
Though Satan meddles, God is in control and can't be
defeated by devilish demoralization
Believers are sealed in Christ with the Holy Spirit which
proves how genuine faith must be
His power works in us to transform us as part of the total
change we'll know in eternity

Raised from the dead, Christ is now the head of the
church—the world's ultimate authority
With the control of everything in hand, God holds the final
triumph, has the final victory
The church should be the full expression of Christ and His
people—He's the Holy Bread
No one should undertake church duties alone; depend on
each other to succeed instead

Believers once walked according to Satan, but Christ's
resurrection conquered the evil one
None is good enough to earn salvation and only in Christ
can we find goodness under the sun
The penalty of sin and its power over us were destroyed by
Christ, so we can stand redeemed
No work we do can bring salvation, but God intends our
salvation to result in a service routine

Jews and Gentiles alike may be full of spiritual pride, but
be purified by Christ, by salvation
For spiritual pride can blind us to our own blemishes and
intensify others miscalculations
But Christ has broken down the barriers of prejudice, so we
can unite with those not like us
For any barrier that can divide fellow believers, the cross
should be our main focus and trust

The church is built upon its spiritual birth, bestowed by the
apostles and prophets of long ago
Not a building, but people in whom Christ lives and reveals
Himself for the world to know
God's family embodies all who believe and therefore can
secure His power when in need
And the love of Christ—its breadth, length, height, and
depth—surpasses all, guaranteed

Believers, called to represent Christ on earth, must live
worthy of the calling they receive
And the gifts given each one are to be used to heighten the
church to spiritually achieve
God's church has a responsibility to build up Christ, to
make disciples of every nation
With everyone utilizing gifts for a specific task, working
together for His glorification

Don't allow human rationalization, excuses or pride to keep
you shunning God and His plan
Don't hold back from God due to ignorance, greed and
callousness that snub His loving hand
Don't cling to the old corrupt self, but slip into the new
which pleases God—rightfully indeed
Don't be driven in a wicked direction, but assume another
way of thinking as the Spirit leads

Those in the Christian walk should dispose of lying, for it
creates conflict and destroys trust
And always deal with anger immediately so that Satan is
given no opportunity to invade us
Refrain from stealing and using foul language, from
bitterness, from clamor and malice, too
Be kind, tender-hearted, and forgiving toward each other,
just as Christ has forgiven you

You who are the light must be reflections of Christ—no
vice, no covetousness, nor idolatry
Let no one deceive you with empty words and condone not
the lifestyle of the world society
Avoid danger zones of darkness and expose those who
attempt to influence you to stray
Live morally—above reproach—so that your life may
reflect onto others along the way

Marriage, like Christ and the church, demands the wife
honor her husband and his leadership
And the husband must sacrifice in order to care for and love
his wife without a mutter or quip
Children should honor their parents so that their life goes
well and they live long on this earth
But fathers mustn't provoke children to anger, but
discipline in love and express their worth

Finally, depend on God's might and use the power of the
Holy Spirit against Satan's schemes
Allow faith to be your shield to protect you from the arrows
and blows of evil's wicked team
Allow prayer to become your lifestyle, praying for all
believers in Christ wherever they may be
Then your life will become a prayer for a world in dire
need of a Savior and Christianity

Read Ephesians and let it strengthen believers and their
Christian unity
Give thanks to God for His church family worldwide and
its diversity
Read Ephesians and pray for the saints—fellow believers
everywhere
Hover over them and nurture your church with strength and
loving care

PHILIPPIANS

Rejoice in the Lord always; again I will say rejoice!
4:4

I can do all things through Him who strengthens me.
4:13

PHILIPPIANS

Paul wrote to the Philippians from prison to thank them for
help in spreading God's Word
Praying they would be able to discern godliness and plant
godly concepts righteously superb
So within the letter, as Paul expresses his love and affection
and the great joy it brings
Let's take a look at how that joy is grounded in Christ alone
and not in earthly things:

Don't allow tragedies in life to hinder you from disclosing
your faith with those you meet
Tough circumstances aren't as important as how we react to
them—is it courage or defeat?
Use those tough times to further the gospel, whether you're
mired in trials and tribulations
And God will breathe triumph from tragedy, poetry from
ashes—such is His reputation

Don't live for money or power, pleasure or prestige, for
fame or worldly prosperity
Live to love, worship and serve—develop eternal values
and spread the gospel universally
Do nothing through selfish ambition or conceit, but regard
others more important than you
Consider Christ is God, yet He didn't dangle His position
as something to flaunt and cling to

He is God, yet appeared as man and was humbly obedient
to the point of death on the cross
Thus, God exalted Him and gave Him a position of might
and dominion for the ultimate cost
So, dear believers, take care to obey God, whether in the
presence of leaders or on your own
His spirit lives there inside to guide and empower you to do
His will in concert or alone

Avoid grumbling and arguing among fellow believers as
you set about doing God's will
So that you reveal that you are above reproach, that you're
blameless, whole and fulfilled
Because as a Christian, you are the light for a corrupt,
wayward and worldly generation
So your life must shine with purity and love—magnifying
others with godly concentration

Most believers are too immersed in their own needs with no
time for Christian devotion
True Christians can always rejoice in the Lord, but beware
of hypocrites and their notions
Life's successes can't compare with a relationship with
Christ—all else is rubbish for sure
Including family, religion, friends, and freedom or
windfalls pocketed on your last detour

When you know Christ, you can let go of your
achievements, failures, sins and liberties
And look ahead to the end of life's race, to the great prize
of holiness—awaiting victory
Imitate Christ, but know many claim Christianity, yet are
enemies of the cross they defame
True believers' citizenship is in heaven and one day will be
glorified forever in His name

Find joy in the Lord; be gentle to all—to believers and
unbelievers show love and care
Don't worry about anything—great or small—but take
everything to the Lord in prayer
And you'll find the peace of God; it will guard your heart
and mind against any anxiety
So when you face any adverse situation, you'll embrace
peace and not find it a mystery

Whatever we deposit into our minds, determines what our
words or actions will be
So whatever is true, noble, just, pure and lovely—infuse
into the mind's memory
Everything of good reputation, excellent, and
praiseworthy—set firmly in your mind
And put into practice God's Word you've read and
digested; put your faith on the line

If you view life from God's prospective, you learn to be
content in any circumstance
Whether you have plenty or you're in need, just draw on
Christ's strength to be enhanced
Then you'll be able do the things God wills—those things
He will empower you to do
For God never calls you to accomplish something without
giving you His blessings, too

He will meet all your needs if you are faithful to Him—if
you give your life and obey
As you trust Him, your attitude and cravings will change—
just let Him have His way
You'll see the difference between wants and needs as your
heart embraces the Perfect One
Accept Him and be filled with His power and, as you live
for Him, pure joy will come

Read Philippians and experience the utter joy which Paul so
plainly expressed
Despite being imprisoned and restrained, he felt gloriously
free and blessed
Read Philippians and experience the freedom of Paul's
enthusiastic heart
Then rejoice with him and live for Christ, come make a
brand new start!

COLOSSIANS

Set your mind on the things above,
not on earthly things.
3:2

Let the peace of God rule in your hearts,
to which indeed you were called in one body;
and be thankful.
3:15

COLOSSIANS

Paul wrote to the Colossians from prison to combat false
teachings in the church
And to show them that all they needed they had in Christ—
no need for further search
Paul set down his greeting, a word of thanksgiving, and a
prayer he faithfully prayed
Declaring great devotion to Christ and unlimited love for
all believers was displayed

Paul prayed they'd gain wisdom, understand God's will and
please Him in all they do
Bear good fruit, grow in a deep knowledge of God and be
filled with His power, too
That they'd endure, be satiated with Christ's joy and give
thanks to the Father above
Noting that God primes us for heaven and the rest of his
letter salutes his faith and love:

True Christians have been delivered from darkness into
light and is no longer in slavery
They have been delivered from guilt to forgiveness, from
Satan to God, and are now set free
Jesus, God's image, reflects and reveals God to us—is
equal to and is God of all creation
All things were created through Him—all rulers and
powers are under His authorization

Christ is the head of the church and was the first to rise
with a body that was glorified
He is the source of all spiritual life, is spiritually supreme in
all things near and wide
Christ as a human being brought about reconciliation by
His horrific death on the cross
His sacrifice was complete, so it's possible to stand before
God with not one spiritual loss

Beware of philosophy that credits humanity, instead of
Christ, for solutions to trials of life
So lest you be deceived, test all teachings to see if they
agree with the teachings of Christ
For there are many traditions of man used for life problems
which dismiss God totally
So keep alert, your eyes Christ-focused, using God's holy
Word to resist such heresy

Don't let anyone judge your diet, religious rites or the
Sabbath you keep for God's pleasure
Or for not adhering to the doctrine of salvation by works,
rather than faith as a measure
Faith is the only way to be saved and though the law shows
us how to obey God dutifully
Instead of focusing on outward observances, focus on
worshiping Christ and on eternity

Don't be like false teachers who delight in false humility
and claim God is far away
Who find pride in bringing praise to self rather than to
God—dismissing Him day after day
Who teach that you have to worship angels in order to
contact God, to make Him evident
That's not Scriptural, so let the Word lead you—not some
false opinion or idle argument

A true believer should not fix his thoughts on earthly
things; rather, look to eternity
Look at life only from God's point of view, not attaching
onto material things temporarily
Christ is our power and He can empower us and give us joy
incomprehensible by men
But one day He'll return for His earthly saints and we'll
stand with Him in glory then

Don't catch the flame of sexual immorality, moral filth,
unbridled lust, or keen desires
Don't yield to greediness which mirrors idolatry as sexual
appetite grows like wildfire
These evil kinds of behavior must be eliminated because
they can utterly destroy you
Rely on the Holy Spirit, so God's judgment doesn't chasten
through and through

Wives and husbands hold a mutual responsibility to submit
and love respectively
Children must obey their parents in everything and God
will bless their integrity
Fathers, do not provoke your children, but discipline firmly
with love and care
And to all, regard your work as an act of worship to God, a
holy attitude you share

Be diligent in prayer, maintain attentiveness to it—giving
thanks for all God bestowed
Be like Paul who asked the Colossians to pray for them in
Rome in a similar mode
Notice that he doesn't ask them to pray for his release;
rather, that his message be heard
That God would open a door for the lost so he might have a
chance to preach the Word

Read Colossians and clearly see that the source of our
spiritual life is Christ alone
If we believe, He'll be our Lord and Savior and live in our
hearts to guide us on and on
Read Colossians and clearly see that works, knowledge or
mysteries offer us no salvation
But only through the Lord Christ Jesus do we ever reach a
true spiritual identification

1 THESSALONIANS

For if we believe that Jesus died and rose again,
even so God will bring with Him
those who have fallen asleep in Jesus.
4:14

Faithful is He who calls you,
and He also will bring it to pass.
5:24

1 THESSALONIANS

Paul's letter to the Thessalonians was written to help make
their faith stronger
And to make sure misconceptions of Christ's return didn't
linger any longer
Paul began by recounting how he and his companions first
brought the good news
How they had welcomed their salvation with joy, while
enduring bruising residues

Paul encouraged the Thessalonians to live lives honorable
to God, holy and upright
And thanked them for accepting God's Word which works
in those who embrace the Light
He reminded them that Jewish Christians were persecuted
by fellow Jews in Jesus' name
Just as Gentile Christians were persecuted by fellow
Gentiles—the reason being the same

Paul sent Timothy to encourage them to stand tough
through all their doubt and adversity
Believers will suffer affliction, but God will generate
growth out of every bit of that misery
Be an encourager, pray for continued maturity, and bring
new believers tirelessly along
Despite temptation and hardship in your walk, remain
steadfast, courageous and strong

He challenged them in their walk to honor and please God
above all—to do it faithfully
To abstain from sexual immorality, love one another, and be
good citizens in society
For loved ones who had died, he gave them comfort by the
promise of resurrection day
Warning them to stay ready because no one knows when
He'll come and have His way

Paul offered the Thessalonians a sprinkling of advice on
how to bunker down and prepare
He urged them to warn the idle, to encourage the
fainthearted, to support the weak with care
To be patient with everyone—showing kindness and love—
to rejoice and pray without cease
To give thanks in everything and not stifle your spiritual
gifts, but encourage their release

Never ridicule anyone who doesn't agree with the Christian
beliefs you know are true
But always test those ideas against the Bible, accept God's
Word, rejecting any false view
Avoid every kind of evil and allow it no stance of any form;
just focus on God and obey
For He who begins a good work in you is faithful and will
complete it on that glorious day

Read 1 Thessalonians and absorb the doable advice Paul
offers for living righteously
And when you're burdened by the cares of the world, look
to the Lord for serenity
Read 1 Thessalonians and absorb the promise which the
return of Christ will bring
Live the gospel as though He's coming this very moment,
grab onto hope and sing!

2 THESSALONIANS

*May the Lord direct your hearts into the love of God
and into the steadfastness of Christ.*
3:5

2 THESSALONIANS

Giving thanks to God and expressing joy because their faith
was making amazing strides
Paul wrote to the Thessalonian believers once again to set
misunderstanding aside
He also commended them for remaining faithful in the
midst of woes and persecution
Their perseverance had caused Paul and his companions to
tell others of their resolution

We who live for Christ will undergo affliction as part of
God's plan for those who believe
But remember we will find relief in our suffering, and
strength from it all will be received
We will also find relief in the knowledge that our suffering
will prepare us for eternity
So when we enter paradise and stand aghast before the
Savior, we'll then be truly free

We must not listen to hearsay and whispers that announce
the day of the Lord has come
But in the meantime, hold onto the truth of the Word and
tell the world of the Perfect One
Trust in God and accept His encouragement, His
everlasting love and promise by grace
Let Him comfort and strengthen your heart as you spread
the gospel from place to place

Make prayer your main defense as you pray for God's
divine power and spread His Word
Pray you will receive refuge and strength against evil so
your mission won't be deterred
Don't associate with the lazy and unruly but offer yourself
up as a holy example to others
Lazy folks waste time and become a burden to the church,
to other sisters and brothers

Do not support anyone financially who persist in their
idleness, so he'll be put to shame
Yet don't treat him as an enemy with coldness or cruelty,
but with compassion in Jesus' name
Pray that this sort of discipline will embarrass and humble
him to mend his ungodly ways
And will restore him back to the Lord, back to God's
people, back to good service days

Read 2 Thessalonians and realize that your faith in God can
evoke affliction
But the reward comes in the morning if you reside in His
holy jurisdiction

1 TIMOTHY

Let no one look down on your youthfulness,
but rather in speech, conduct, love, faith, and purity,
show yourself an example of those who believe.
4:12

1 TIMOTHY

Paul wrote to Timothy in Ephesus to encourage and counsel
him on church issues of heresy
Warning him that the false teachers were motivated by their
own interests, not Christianity
Paul advised him to steer clear of their fruitless religious
controversies and speculations
Because their useless discussions distract from the gospel,
from good news communication

Those false teachers wanted to be teachers of the law, yet
did not understand its intention
The law is good if used to show believers their sin; then
lead them to godly comprehension
It's for the rebellious, the unholy, murderers, immoral men
and homosexual sinners, too
It's for kidnappers, liars, false witnesses—for those adverse
to a sound and practical view

So hold fast to your faith in Christ and do not feel guilty for
horrific sins of the past
No matter how heinous your history, God wants to forgive
you and use your life at last
Just as Paul had once sneered at Christ, had hunted down
and murdered Christians, too
God had mercy, forgave him and used him and He longs to
do the very same for you

Pray for each other, for your government leaders, for
people around the world in authority
Honest prayer is good in God's sight and offers your life a
sweet stroke of joyous harmony
Therefore, pray and lift up holy hands, but not if you hold
fast to any anger and dissension
And don't try to gain respect by fine attire; rather, by being
godly, not by seeking attention

Leaders bear a heavy responsibility to oversee the church,
read the Word and live righteously
Therefore, pastors and church leaders must be above
reproach, not inundated in adultery
They must be gentle, prudent, respectable, hospitable,
teachable and not addicted to wine
They must be aggressive, but peaceful and free from love of
money—that's the bottom line

A church leader must manage his home well—teach and
discipline his children with dignity
He must not be a convert who isn't yet secure and strong,
and grounded in the faith solidly
A church leader must have a good reputation with
unbelievers, so that Satan can't ensnare
Women as well must be dignified and modest with no
gossiping and faithful beyond compare

Church leaders must be aware that some will desert the
faith, some will deceive and lie
Some will allow evil to indwell them and will encourage
others to follow their demonic ties
Their conscience becomes insensitive and callous,
distorting Christian truth with hypocrisy
So believers must guard against teachings that contradict
the Bible in any aspect that might be

Pastors, discipline yourselves to be godly, using your gifts
to serve and honor God each day
No matter if you're young, your conduct and speech, your
faith and purity will have much to say
As a believer, you are an example; therefore, live so others
can clearly see Christ in you
As you attend to studying the Word, to teaching and to
admonishing whenever there is need to

Pastors, be careful not to rebuke the elderly and toward the
young don't attempt to domineer
Treat women with dignity and if widows have no family
support, let the church then appear
The elders who work hard at their duties should be
considered worthy of honor and esteem
Accusations against those elders who sin require two or
three witnesses present on the scene

When dealing with discipline in the church always avoid
any prejudice, avoid any partiality
Never be hasty in choosing leaders lest you neglect crucial
problems of sin you may not see
So choose church leaders carefully, allowing time to permit
the good or the bad to ensue
For if you don't judge on first impression, eventually their
true character will shine through

Once again, be aware of those espousing strange doctrines
which disagree with God's Word
They're conceited, know nothing and use godliness as a
money-making scheme that's absurd
But real godliness—being satisfied with your own faith—is
worth more than money can buy
Because our hands were empty at birth and will be empty
when we breathe our last and die

So be content with what you have because yearning to be
rich can lead into temptation
For the love of money is the source of all kinds of evil and
results in definite damnation
Flee from what isn't right, godly, faithful, lovely, enduring,
and gentle along the way
Stay the course and run well in the race of faith, cling to
eternity, living holy day by day

Keep God's commandments, your testimony blemish-free,
without a trace of disgrace
When Christ returns to reign upon the earth, you'll know
He is King when you see His face
He alone is immortal and surrounded by the splendor of
glory, He alone is our authority
He alone is the Light; honor and everlasting dominion
belong to Him, and shall always be

The rich carry a huge responsibility not to be conceited or
arrogant because of their prosperity
They must be cautious not to put their hope in money rather
than in God who can set them free
They must be rich in good deeds and love, full of
generosity and always ready to share
And must use their riches for God's work today to realize
heaven's precious aftercare

Protect the truth of the gospel which is entrusted to you by
God who called you to this place
And avoid worldly and empty talk about worthless matters
which have no valuable base
Avoid false teachings with contrary arguments testifying as
truth but opposing Christianity
For any hypotheses which refute the Bible should be duly
shunned and rejected immediately

Read 1 Timothy and note that church leaders must ensure
that Christianity is preserved
By opposing false teachers, by teaching sound doctrine—
being Christ-like and in the Word
Read 1 Timothy and note that, after passing of time, church
leaders must be chosen carefully
To make certain they're fully committed to Christ and have
matured in Him with tenacity

2 TIMOTHY

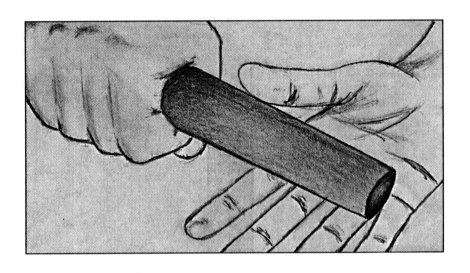

Be diligent to present yourself approved to God as a workman who does not need to be ashamed, accurately handling the word of truth.
2:15

All Scripture is God-breathed.
3:16a

I have fought the good fight, I have finished the race, I have kept the faith.
4:7

2 TIMOTHY

Paul would soon be executed and wrote to Timothy, his
very dear friend
He wanted to give him final counsel before his life met its
imminent end
Timothy was like a son to him, whom he had mentored
diligently along the way
So in this last letter, he passes the torch to him to stand as a
leader of his day

Paul reminded Timothy to persevere and use his spiritual
gifts to enhance God's light
For God gives Christians power, purpose, love, and
discipline to fight the good fight
Therefore, fear not to testify for the Lord—even in
suffering—for the gospel has no shame
Because God, your refuge, equips you with resources to
face today and tomorrow the same

Keep your eyes on Christ and don't try to live for him in
your own strength alone
You'll endure despite the suffering because victory awaits
you at the Master's throne
Be perceptive to God's Word and apply it to your life in
everything you say or do
Remember Jesus displayed God's nature in human form,
yet lived without sin too

Do not argue over insignificant or worldly matters; it incites
anger and causes ill-will
Do not put yourself above God, but be one with His Word
in order to be fulfilled
Keep your life pure, flee from lustful temptation and pursue
love and righteousness
In teaching truth, be kind, gentle, patient and respectful,
and you'll meet with success

Make most of the time God has given you and yield not to
the pressures of society
Don't settle for comfort without commitment and stand
against evil—living righteously
Rely on the Scriptures—build up your faith through the
Word, expanding it day by day
Use it as a safeguard against false teaching and as a guide
to take action God's way

Preach the Gospel so that Christianity can spread for those
existing without salvation
Being forever ready to serve God, to grasp opportunities to
obey Him in any situation
Keep your head about you in all things, persevere in
hardships and realize your ministry
Do not react quickly when people or circumstances agitate
you—but act responsibly

All these things Paul wrote to Timothy as his time
diminished and neared its end
To give encouragement and godly advice in this last
message to his very dear friend
Paul had fought the good fight, had finished the course, had
kept the faith too
So now God would bring him safely home to experience a
joy he never knew

Read 2 Timothy and reflect: Was there ever another disciple
like the missionary Paul?
With great depth of faith, undying love and tenacious
conviction—oh, how he stood tall!
Read 2 Timothy and reflect: Paul was inspired by the Holy
Spirit to spread God's Word
His constant hope and profound insight exposed his life and
his priorities weren't deferred

Read 2 Timothy and reflect on his last words to his friend
then, and now to us all
Then rededicate yourself to God and His Word, to changing
lives just like Paul
Read 2 Timothy and reflect: What living legacy will you
leave to flourish and endure?
Is there a Timothy in your life today who can keep the
Gospel alive and secure?

TITUS

The reason I left you in Crete
was that you might straighten out
what was left unfinished
and appoint elders in every town,
as I directed you.
1:5

TITUS

Like Timothy, Paul had also nurtured Titus in Christian
ways and in church responsibility
So he wrote this letter to Titus in order to continue the
mentoring process progressively
To counsel him on his duty of church leadership and of
overseeing the churches of Crete
On teaching only the Word, appointing and training elders
to make the churches complete

Choose those who are above reproach, those who are living
out God's Word every day
And be on guard for those who teach false doctrines and
lead others purposely astray
Those who are in Christ discover goodness and purity even
amidst evil, high and low
But those who are corrupt and unbelieving find evil in
anything wherever they may go

Older men in the church need to exhibit godly behavior—
need wisdom and discernment
And young men must be mindful of the Christian design,
must pursue it by being obedient
Because Christ died and rescued us from sin, believers are
freed from sin's awful sting
So deny ungodliness and worldly desires, living prudently
and righteously in everything

Christians must obey their government and all its civil
regulations, laws and authorities
Striving to be good citizens no matter where they are—
that's a Christian's responsibility
Remember, in the past, believers pursued a life of pleasure
and caved in to fleshly desires
But Christ saved them from a life full of sin and their new
life must be Christ-inspired

Avoid foolish controversies, quarreling and such which
greatly threaten a church's unity
And a man who has been warned twice for his evilness
must be rejected immediately
Because this man is tainted, is sinning and knows it, but
refuses steps to restoration
So his discipline is warranted, but must be dispensed with
love as well as condemnation

Read Titus and see Paul helping a young man grow into a
church leader of his day
See him being trained in Christian principles for structuring
the church in a godly way
Read Titus and see a Christian leader maturing in Christian
responsibility
All because someone inspired him and prepared him to
endure his ministry

PHILEMON

Perhaps the reason he was
separated from you for a little while
was that you might have him back for good—
no longer as a slave, but better than a slave,
as a dear brother.
He is very dear to me but even dearer to you,
both as a man and as a brother in the Lord.
(15-16)

PHILEMON

Onesimus was a slave who belonged to Paul's friend
Philemon in Colossae
He had run away and had traveled to Rome where he met
Paul eventually
While Paul was under house arrest, he had led Onesimus to
salvation, into the Light
Now Paul had to convince Philemon to accept him back—
not as a slave in his sight

So Paul wrote to Philemon to convince him to forgive the
slave in Christian love
And he appealed to his personal commitment as a believer
in the Lord above
For now both men were members of God's family—both
equal one to the other
Because in Christ no difference exists; every believer is a
sister or brother

Paul showed his love for Onesimus by guaranteeing to
repay any amount he owed
And reminded Philemon how he once led him to Christ, to
salvation's righteous road
In hopes that his heart would open wide and let the wall
become a piece of the past
With no barrier between master and slave, but the two
united as one in Christ at last

Read Philemon and notice that true Christians forgive and
possess open minds
And there exist only one family in Christ, no matter one's
status or kind
Read Philemon and notice a deep manifestation of Christ's
truth and power
And genuine Christian fellowship in which unity embodies
every golden hour

HEBREWS

*And He is the radiance of His glory
and the exact representation of His nature,
and upholds all things by the word of His power.
When He had made purification of sins,
He sat down at the right hand
of the Majesty on high.
1:3*

*Jesus Christ is the same yesterday and today and forever.
13:8*

HEBREWS

Hebrews was written to those Jewish Christians who found
the Gospel hard to accept
Who had been grounded in their traditional ways of
Judaism in which the law was kept
So the motive of this message was to prove that Christ is
better, Christianity supreme
To reassure them Christ is absolutely sufficient for
salvation because you're redeemed

In Old Testament times, God used different people to relay
His messages through prophecy
Speaking in visions, dreams and personal communication,
God revealed His will explicitly
The Jewish people accepted the Old Testament expressed
through worship and dedication
The commandments, rituals and prophets set the path to
forgiveness with God's inspiration

But it was difficult for them to accept that God revealed
Himself through Christ His Son
Who conquered sin, fulfilled the law and prophecy, and
shattered barriers to the Holy One
Who provided a way to eternity, whose sacrifice was final,
who is superior to all creation
For there is none greater than He, now or ever, because
Jesus is God without qualification

Jesus is not God's highest angel as many false teachers
taught in the early church days
Angels do not exist to be worshiped, but Jesus alone is
worthy of that sort of praise
Angels are spirits whom God created as His messengers to
serve under His authority
But Jesus is the foundation and He is God—changeless,
just, merciful, our true security

Heed the truth of the Scriptures as you focus on Christ and
His life; then resolve to obey
So you won't become entangled in false teachings, lose
spiritual focus, thus lose your way
Jesus is Lord over all and God purposely placed Him on
earth as ransom for our iniquity
And through His suffering, He completed the course
necessary for our salvation eternally

Believers have the same Father as Jesus and therefore are
His sisters and brothers as well
And because of His death and resurrection, believers
needn't fear death's morbid tale
Realizing His temptations and excruciating pain at Calvary
can help us carry our cross
So run to Him for strength and endurance, and trust Him—
the one who paid the cost

As the focal figure of faith, Jesus is worthy of greater honor
than prophets or anyone
For prophets were only God's human servants, but Jesus is
God who came as His son
When we persist in refusing to believe in God, He will
leave us alone to wallow in our sin
Then lacking a new heart, mind and spirit, God's best is
prohibited from coming in

With the power to change lives, God's Word is living,
mighty and clearly communicates
It can pierce the marrow of our souls, so make it your daily
bread—allow it to penetrate
Nothing is hidden from God; He knows all we think, sees
all we do—He is everywhere
Our lives are wide open to Him and He loves us dearly,
though too often we are unaware

To the Jews, the high priest represented the sole supreme
religious authority of the land
But Jesus' authority is sovereign, infinite, and mighty for
He came as God and man
And unlike the high priest, Jesus forever sits at God's right
hand available to intercede
To hear our prayers as He mediates between us and God—
His intercession guaranteed

Those who taste the love of God, who come close to
salvation and then turn away
Have closed their hearts, rejected Christ and will not be
saved from judgment day
They dismiss God who is truth and who promises us that
He will keep us secure
They dismiss His unconditional love, His forgiveness of
sin—His help to endure

When Jesus died for our sin, once and for all animal
sacrifice was brought to an end
Because Christ is the perfect, final sacrifice and serves as
the perfect atonement for sin
So no longer was there need for priests who accepted
offerings for one's forgiveness
Jesus is now high priest, and sin—past, present and
future—is forgiven if confessed

Within the tabernacle, in Old Testament days, the holy of

holies was veiled from view
Only the high priest could enter that holy place to offer
one's sacrifice for sin when due
He did this only once a year, on the Day of Atonement,
which covered sin temporarily
But Jesus' death eliminated the veil, so now we can talk to
God in public or in privacy

Now we can draw near to Him for personal access without
any rigid kind of design
With a channel to God through Christ to build a
relationship with Him and not be confined
Believers should worship together, share their faith,
strengthen and encourage one another
For as each day passes, we come closer to His return for
His Christian sisters and brothers

Truly believe that God is exactly who He says He is and
will do what He says He will do
He will fulfill His promises if we manifest our faith in Him,
and make us brand new
Because without faith it is impossible to please God and
receive your heavenly treasure
Consider Noah, Abraham and Moses who acted on faith
and heightened God's pleasure

Your faith can deliver momentous victories or severe
torment, even deliver death silently
Having a sound faith in God does not guarantee a life that's
sunny, affluent or carefree
Quite the contrary, most likely your faith guarantees you
meet some sort of mistreatment
While on earth, the purpose for the suffering may never be
realize, but it is heaven-sent

Being a Christian entails hard work and necessitates giving
up worldly, fleshly things
Requiring you to run the race, to struggle against sin with
the power the Holy Spirit brings
Through all the trials and tribulations, keep your focus on
Christ, for if you glance away
You'll stumble and fall, so as you head home keep Him in
sight every moment of the day

When all else is crumbling around you, only God's
kingdom will remain firm and stand
No matter what happens here on earth, a solid foundation
will solidify your future's hand
For when your life is built on Christ, your future is secure
in a kingdom that's unshakable
And your faith will withstand any fire or storm as you look
toward God who is unbreakable

Show love to fellow believers, and to strangers do not
neglect to display hospitality
To those who are in prison and those who have been
mistreated, show them empathy
Honor your marriage vows and for whatever you have be
thankful with contentment
And let your love reach such depths until it touches others
with great heartfelt intent

Do not become attached to this world because our lives and
possessions are temporary
Don't store up your treasures here, but store them in heaven
where you'll find eternity
Because only your relationship with God and your service
to Him will linger forever
So let nothing hinder you from complete loyalty to
Christ—dismiss your Lord never

Read Hebrews and vow now to let Christian maturity begin
Make Christ the beginning of your faith and make Him the end
Read Hebrews and vow to center your life solely on the King
Because He's better than any fascination on earth, anyone
or anything

JAMES

The tongue is a fire, the very world of iniquity;
the tongue is set among our members
as that which defiles the entire body,
and sets on fire the course of our life,
and is set on fire by hell.
3:6

JAMES

James wrote to some of the early Jewish Christians to teach
proper Christian behavior
To disclose hypocrisy and teach that the test of faith is a
changed life through the Savior
Saying you will experience tough times, but turn them into
advantageous times to learn
Trials will test your faith and give rise to perseverance and
a positive perspective in turn

Even though God will test you, He will never tempt you by
enticing you into sin
When you're confronted with sin, just obey the Word and
you'll resist temptation's spin
Eliminate anything in your life that reeks of evil and
humble yourself to receive salvation
Don't just listen to God's Word; obey it by putting into
action that Biblical information

The attitude of showing favoritism toward the well-to-do
and ignoring the pauper is sin
Just recognize that both are in need of Christ and His love,
no matter the status they're in
Don't choose to keep only part of God's law and shove the
rest of His standards aside
God's grace doesn't erase your responsibility to obey—the
Holy Spirit within is fortified

You cannot be a Christian by merely agreeing with Biblical
truths; commitment is the key
Every part of your being must be committed to Christ—
your heart, mind and soul totally
Your good works can't ever earn salvation; rather, good
works exist as faith's offspring
An affirmation of your faith in Christ must step forward,
not some substitute for anything

The tongue is wildfire, can do great damage and spread
destruction around expeditiously
Don't be careless with what you say because idle, hateful
words leave scars that never flee
True wisdom comes from above and can be measured by
your words and by how you act
It is peaceful, gentle, reasonable, persevering, and
forgiving—without hypocrisy, in fact

Quarrels and conflict are the result of evil desires which
wrestle and tussle inside us
More money! More possessions! More recognition! Lofty
status! Many grab, many lust
You don't get because you don't ask; you ask and don't
receive because of wicked intent
Seeking pleasure at the expense of others, at the expense of
disobeying God is unintelligent

Pride produces egotism and greed, over and above the
things you really and truly need
It drives you to believe you deserve everything you see or
everything you imagine indeed
But you can be delivered from your selfishness by
humbling yourself before the Lord
Then you'll realize that worldly enticements are mere
substitutes for God's eternal reward

With the Holy Spirit inside as your power source, you're
able to resist the devil and he'll flee
Submit to God's control and lead a pure, holy life as you
repent for your sins with humility
Humble yourself before God—let His power guide you—
and He will exalt you immeasurably
In spite of your human failings, He'll reach out and shower
you with love, hope and dignity

Riches are worthless treasures that will be useless, will be
futile when Christ returns
So spend your days storing up treasures that will be
profitable to eternity's concern
The love of money, not money itself, leads to evil as more
and more of it you pursue
And in order to acquire more, some persecute others and
greed comes shining through

Wait patiently for Christ's return; but while you wait, there
is much work to be done
Live by faith, advance His kingdom, and look to eternity
while the race is being run
Do not lie or judge others for their frailties, in order that
you may not be judged too
Christ is the judge and when He returns, none will
escape—He'll issue their just due

Church members should pray for each other and count on
them for support and prayer
Pray in faith for the sick, for anyone who has committed
sin, for any burden hard to bear
Confess your sins to one another and let prayer be the very
first approach for any need
Pray earnestly and ceaselessly, help backsliders repent,
seek forgiveness guaranteed

Read James and behold faith in action among true
Christians—the holy heavyweights
As it calls you to commitment, to become a doer of the
Word as God so designates
Read James and behold how believers must be examples of
heaven here on earth
As they live God's Word each day, drawing others to
salvation and to a brand new birth

1 PETER

Now to you who believe, this stone is precious.
But to those who do not believe,
"The stone the builders rejected,
has become the capstone,"
and,
"A stone that causes men to stumble
and a rock that makes them fall."
They stumble because they disobey the message—
which is also what they were destined for.
2:7-8

1 PETER

The apostle Peter wrote to the Jewish Christians who were
being oppressed
To encourage them as they were scattered and as they
suffered in distress
To remind them that their inheritance in eternity means
secure reservations
And through trials, their faith can survive by God's power
and their dedication

Trials will refine your faith, burn away impurities and
prepare you for eternity
Trials will teach patience and surely mature you into what
God wants you to be
So live holy lives by imitating God's standards, devoted in
everything you do
Let the Holy Spirit be your counselor to help you triumph
over sin and its residue

Yearn to grow in the Lord, and you will need Him more
and more—so be diligent
Then as your spiritual appetite swells, you'll mature with
His divine nourishment
The church is God's house, Christ the cornerstone, each
member a stone concertedly
Which means the church is the body, Christ the head, and
believers members in unity

Believers are "aliens and strangers" in this world because
this is not their real home
Their real home is with God in heaven where life is eternal
there before His throne
But while on earth, submit to civil authority and to your
employer—to both do obey
Do this "for the sake of the Lord" so that His gospel will be
respected in every way

If you suffer because of your faith, remember Christ
suffered, yet never once sinned
While being ridiculed, He never ridiculed in return, blew
not one threat in the wind
Rather, He kept relying on the Father for strength and
endurance, for hope and security
In order that we be forgiven our sins, He suffered and died
on the cross at Calvary

Wives mustn't be unduly engrossed in appearance, but
develop inner beauty instead
Which—precious in God's sight—should exude from the
heart and not from the head
Husbands, be understanding and respectful of your wives
so prayers won't be barred
For if a man uses his position to mistreat his wife, his
kinship with God will be scarred

Strive to enrich your relationship with God and respond to
another's needs willingly
Treat each other as sister and brother, being lovingly
sensitive and as caring as can be
Believers must be willing to encourage each other and
delight in each other's success
And repay wrong done to them by praying for the offender
and be mightily blessed

Always be prepared and willing to do God's bidding and to
suffer for it if necessary
Just focus on Christ and obey His will and the end of sin's
power becomes legendary
When you have a changed life, friends may show contempt
and blatantly put you down
Resist such pressure by finding encouragement from
believers who stand on solid ground

Be grateful that you're given the privilege to suffer for
Christ, rejoice through the ordeal
You'll be blessed doing His will, so don't be ashamed of
your faith and commit with zeal
God is faithful and those who suffer due to the will of God
shall find utter and perfect peace
Because He can see the trials you endure and you can count
on Him for heavenly release

Church elders must care for the people and lead from a
desire to serve, not out of obligation
They must be interested in giving, not in what they can get
from their prominent station
They must be models and lead by example, not by force or
some other fallacious reason
And mustn't use their leadership as a position of power, but
for service in every season

Youth should submit to their elders; and no matter the age,
be humble to serve one another
Be humble enough to admit that the upstarts and the elders
can learn much from each other
Throw yourself at God's feet; place your anxieties upon
Him and your burdens He will bear
He will carry the weight of your struggles and deliver you
at last into eternity's care

Read 1 Peter and remember that when you suffer for doing
what is right
Recall the price Jesus Christ our Savior paid and commit to
Him in your fight
When you're persecuted for your faith, rejoice in your great
oppression
Rejoice that you're worthy to suffer for Him for your
Christian expressions

Read 1 Peter and remember that trials refine your belief
So remain devoted to God and His joy will bring heavenly relief

2 PETER

*But false prophets also arose among the people,
just as there will also be false teachers among you,
who will secretly introduce destructive heresies,
even denying the Master who brought them,
bringing swift destruction upon themselves.*

2:1

2 PETER

Peter wrote to fellow Christians to warn them of false
teachers and their heresy
To refute their evil intentions and reaffirm the supremacy of
truths of Christianity
Peter also wrote to warn them of imminent danger of
complacency within
To remind them to rely on the Word, put faith first, and
look to Christ to come again

The remedy for stagnation among believers is to draw
closer to God each day
To raise the level of perseverance, do God's will as you
love others in a godly way
Work hard to verify your faith by developing Christ-like
qualities in all you say or do
Remember salvation isn't based on hard work, but will
result in acts of service by you

Beware of false teachers who contradict the Bible—their
message is not from the Lord
Until Christ returns, let the Scripture and the Holy Spirit
guide you into God's accord
There will be false teachers among you who will distort the
gospel with deadly heresy
Even deny Jesus, discredit His life, death and
resurrection—saying that couldn't be

These false teachers might do or say anything for money
with their lies and awful greed
They slander any godly truths they don't understand and
Satan's power they misread
They do whatever they feel like doing and claim only what
can be seen is absolutely real
They are boastful fools who promote evil and lead others
away from Christ and His will

If you were once saved and later rejected God and then
returned to your usual sinfulness
You are worst off than before, rejecting the only one who
will forgive your sorry mess
If Christ reaches out His hand to you and you refuse to grab
it, to walk that holy road
You have cast aside your only means of escape from Satan
and assumed a gruesome load

In the last days, mockers will come and contend that Jesus
is never coming back
But God is not slow; he just doesn't operate on our
timetable, on our dubious track
He is patient toward us because He doesn't want anyone to
perish because of sin
Rather, He desires everyone to repent, to turn toward Him
and live the way He intends

Christ's second coming will be quick and devastating for
those who do not believe
But if your heart beats for Him, you will not be surprised—
your heart will be relieved
So put your trust in what is eternal and don't be bound to
earth's fleeting treasures
Look toward the restoration of a new heaven and earth—
live to give God the pleasure

Be diligent in ensuring that God sees you as peaceful, pure,
and without blame
And continue to be careful of false teachers who twist the
Scripture in His name
Become more and more Christ-like each day, learning more
and more of His ways
Realize the world will challenge your faith, no matter the
mark of your spiritual days

Read 2 Peter and heed his warning of those who dare to
claim authenticity
Who panhandle for attention and pretend to give Christ
divine courtesy
Read 2 Peter and heed his reminder that the truth of the
gospel does not waver
And take his advice to mature in your faith and in the
knowledge of the Savior

1 JOHN

We love, because He first loved us.
4:19

I write these things to you
who believe in the name of the Son of God
so that you may know that you have eternal life.
5:13

1 JOHN

When the church faces declining commitment, as believers
wander aimlessly
They fall short of standing up for Christ and that puts their
faith in jeopardy
This was the case when John wrote this letter to some
church congregations
To correct errors by false teachers, to stress faith, to
encourage without hesitation

Christ, who came into this world as a human, brought light
and life to one and all
He is eternal and so believers possess eternal life and
should take heart and stand tall
Believers should fellowship with other believers; that's
God's Word—His authority
Which is give-and-take and relies on unity of believers in
social and spiritual harmony

God is Light, perfect and holy—and only He can lead us
out of the depth of sin
His light lays bare—good or bad—whatever situation our
present life operates in
If we desire a relationship with God, we must remove our
sinful ways and commit
If we claim we belong to Him, but proceed to live for
ourselves, we are hypocrites

If we say we are Christians, but see no need to confess our
sins—no need to repent
That really means we think we have no sin, so we deceive
ourselves into devilment
If we confess our sins, He will forgive them and cleanse us
from all unrighteousness
But if we say we have no sin, we are calling God a liar and
His Word we dispossess

Christ is our defender who has already paid the price, who
has suffered the penalty
He is mediator between us and God, and His death satisfied
God's anger at sin totally
If we know Him and don't keep His commandments, we're
liars of the highest class
But if we keep His Word, His love will abide and blaze our
path to eternity at last

One who says He is a Christian, yet despises others and
treats them with disrespect
Cannot grow spiritually because love is the identifying
mark of Christians in all aspects
Obey Christ wholeheartedly and always be concerned about
the well-being of others
When we choose to love mankind, God helps us express
love to our sisters and brothers

Antichrists are false teachers who pretend to be Christians,
but really don't belong
Weak Christians fall prey to them and get lured away
because they're not very strong
You might have heard that just before the world ends, one
great antichrist will arise
But you won't be deceived if you let the Holy Spirit reveal
the distortions he'll devise

True Christians are members of God's family who are
merging, becoming His reflection
As they grow, they learn to be victorious over sin, with
Christ and His perfect direction
But they will be filled with love, will serve others, and will
become very secure in Him
For even if they might allow their conscience to damn their
souls, God will not condemn

We shouldn't believe everything we hear or read, even if we
hear it's God-inspired
Test it against the Bible to see if it's consistent with God's
Word, with His desires
False teachers are drawn to the world because they tell
people what they want to hear
People don't want to see their sins exposed or heed the
demand that their sins disappear

Christ, our model of what love means, was love in
everything He did in life and death
Now the Holy Spirit within believers gives them power to
love with every single breath
God created people to love and He cares deeply for us and
loves us unconditionally
He gave us free will, freedom to choose, for He desires
loving responses with sincerity

Christ died because God's love for us caused Him to search
for a solution to our sin
Now we can receive eternal life because God's love
exposed itself forever without end
Though we've never seen God, if we surrender, He'll be
manifest inside to keep us strong
Then we can face judgment day when all our sins cease and
we'll be where we belong

As a part of God's family, Christians must perceive fellow
believers as sisters and brothers
And welcome the discipline and sweat needed to serve
Christ, loving Him above all others
If we believe in the Son of God, we'll have eternal life; if
we don't, we will miss eternity
And if we believe in Him, God hears our prayers and
responds to our prayers perfectly

If a Christian sees other brothers or sisters commit a sin,
always lift them up in prayer
Ask God to forgive them and pray for their faith in serving
God with joyfulness to spare
The believer is safe from Satan's clutch, but the unbeliever
is chained in woeful slavery
For unless you surrender to Christ, your only choice is to
obey Satan and his depravity

Read 1 John and understand that false teachers lie in
ambush near and far
Don't be baited by their traps, just let God's Word be your
guiding star
Read 1 John and understand how real God—through faith
in Christ—can be
And grasp the certainty that when you believe in Him, you
possess eternity

2 JOHN

And this is love,
that we walk according to His commandments.
This is the commandment,
just as you have heard from the beginning,
that you should walk in it.
(6)

2 JOHN

Truth and love is the foundation for God's people who
believe
Love is obeying God's commandments, but now don't be
deceived
Because false teachers are abundant and lie in wait all over
the earth
They distort truth and sabotage Christ, His doctrine and His
worth

Be careful that you hold onto truth as you serve Him
tirelessly
And it will bring you a bountiful reward for all your
tenacity
Don't be hospitable to false teachers; that will encourage
their dissension
For if you welcome them, you are participating in their evil
intention

Read 2 John and know that the Bible is God's Word
exclusively
It's the only truth and must be obeyed by followers of
Christianity
Read 2 John and know that love is Christianity's true
foundation
And believers mustn't give false teachers an arena to spew
their fabrication

3 JOHN

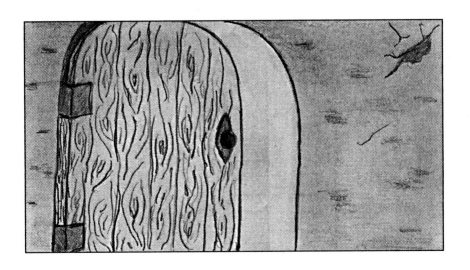

Beloved, you are acting faithfully
in whatever you accomplish for the brethren,
and especially when they are strangers.
(5)

3 JOHN

John wrote to Gaius to thank him for his genuine
hospitality
Which he showed toward traveling Christian teachers and
missionaries
And to encourage him to continue to practice those loving
expressions
So spreaders of the gospel may reach others basking in
transgressions

But unlike Gaius, John denounced Diotrephes and his
dominating demeanor
Who wanted to control the church, to barge in as a coercive
counterfeit leader
He didn't care to associate with other leaders and slandered
them mercilessly
Refusing to welcome those of the gospel, he banished any
opposing his brutality

Do not imitate what is wicked, but reflect the good, what is
of the LORD above
Such as Demetrius, held in high esteem, who mirrored
God's truth and love
Whose character and teachings John had witnessed and for
which he testified
In this letter to Gaius, when John mentioned Demetrius, the
truth was given eyes

Read 3 John and see how important it is not to show
hospitality to false teachers
But to continue to show kindness to true Christians,
missionaries and preachers
Kindness to those travelers who are faithfully spreading
God's Word in ministry
Then you become like a partner in their service—a part of
furthering eternity

JUDE

Beloved, while I was making every effort to write you
about our common salvation,
I felt the necessity to write to you
appealing that you contend earnestly for the faith
which was once for all handed down to the saints.
For certain persons have crept in unnoticed,
those who were long beforehand
marked out for this condemnation,
ungodly persons who turn the grace of our God
into licentiousness
and deny our Master and Lord, Jesus Christ.
(3-4)

JUDE

Jude wrote to believers to remind them to be on guard
constantly
Because opposition would come to pollute their faith with
ugly heresy
These false teachers would snub God's truths, dealing
Christ their rejection
But believers must strive fervently for the faith to retain a
godly complexion

Perceive God as a just God; He will rescue you, but will
punish if need be
Remember the children of Israel, though delivered out of
Egypt and set free
Refused to trust God and with their rebelliousness, there
was no reprieve
So they weren't allowed to enter the promised land because
they didn't believe

Or consider Sodom and Gomorrah where the people
wallowed in sin
So God wiped them off the face of the earth, never to be
seen again
Sinners who don't confess their sins to God will face
eternal separation
If you rebel against Him, if you deny Him, you'll face
eternal damnation

Now consider false teachers who boasted of having
knowledge of God secretly
Which, though difficult for humans to understand, said it
gave them authority
But consider further that God's nature may be beyond our
human comprehension
But through Christ Jesus, He chose to reveal Himself in
order to get our attention

False teachers possess attitudes—like Cain, Balaam and
Korah of the Old Testament
Murder to revenge, prophesy from greed, rebel for power—
all Biblical incidents
Which can result from egotism, jealousy, greed and lust—
ignoring God's will
Typical attitudes of false teachers—sheep in wolves'
clothing, all with false zeal

In the end times there will be mockers who will ridicule
Christ's name
And pursue their unrighteous lust without any
embarrassment or shame
They'll cause division in the church and embrace the world
their own way
But believers must heighten their faith to the utmost and
ceaselessly pray

Have mercy on some sinners by witnessing to them with
love and gentle kindness
Save others as if yanking them from the eternal fire of
hell—so sad, so unblessed
Have mercy on others with fear, hating their immoral acts,
hating their awful sin
Unbelievers need salvation, therefore—no matter their
misdeeds—witness again and again

God will keep believers from falling prey to false teachers
everywhere
If they trust Him and are grounded in Him, they need not
fear or despair
Because He will keep them from stumbling and in Him find
security
And when they see Him face to face, they will be perfect—
sinless eternally

Read Jude and recognize that heresies and temptations truly
do abound
But if believers remain firm in their faith, God will be their
sacred ground
Read Jude and recognize the necessity for opposing any
and all heresy
Defending God's truth at all costs is a Christian's distinct
responsibility

REVELATION

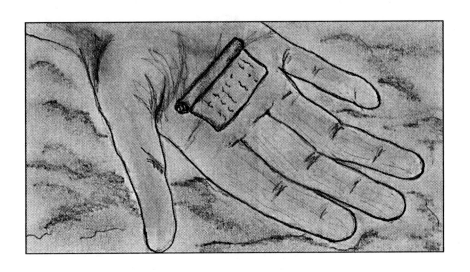

*Blessed is he who reads
and those who hear the words of the prophecy,
and heed the things which are written in it;
for the time is near.*
1:3

*"And He will wipe away every tear from their eyes;
and there will no longer be any death;
there will no longer be any mourning, or crying or pain;
the first things have passed away."*
21:4

"Behold, I am coming quickly,
and My reward is with Me,
to render to every man
according to what he has done."
22:12

REVELATION

The apostle John was nearing his end when a vision from
Christ was unfurled
It disclosed Christ's absolute identity and God's plan for
the end of the world
John wrote of his vision to seven churches in Asia as was
Jesus' clear direction
It centered on Christ's return and triumph, His Kingdom
established with perfection

To the church in Ephesus, Jesus commended them for hard
work and perseverance
For not tolerating sin, for discerning and testing claims of
false apostles' interference
For enduring adversity for His sake and for not becoming
discouraged in time
But the one area of failure He pointed out was that their
love for God had declined

Therefore, the church had to repent of its sin and do what it
did at first to succeed
Still Jesus applauded the church at Ephesus for hating the
Nicolaitans' sinful deeds
And to those who believe, who'd overcome, they'll eat of
the tree of life in Paradise
Where there will be no more sin and where Christ's victory
will finally be realized

To the church in Smyrna, Jesus noted their faith through
poverty and persecution
And encouraged them not to fear, but to remain faithful to
God—life's only solution
To be faithful, even though they would have tribulations,
and stand until death
Because at the end of life, His promise of eternity will
breathe an eternal breath

To the church in Pergamum—which was surrounded by
worshipers of idolatry
Jesus commended them for standing against influences—
temptations of that society
But He rebuked them for tolerating heresy and immorality
amidst Christians there
For believers must never compromise their faith for any
reason, anytime, anywhere

To the church in Thyatira, Jesus hailed them for their
growth in enacting good deeds
But reprimanded them for shutting their eyes to a woman
whose aim was to mislead
Because she taught others to believe that sexual immorality
wasn't a serious concern
And she was not willing to repent and recommit to Christ—
just refused to ever turn

To the church in Sardis, Jesus observed that He knew of
their empty operation
That He knew spiritual death was their problem, despite an
active reputation
So He urged the church to repent and turn to God, the only
spiritual and divine key
And the names of the few faithful would remain in the book
of life for their purity

To the church in Philadelphia, Jesus specified their
faithfulness and their endurance
And promised to spare them from the hour of testing—that
was their assurance
He encouraged them to hold onto their strength of purpose
and always persevere
Because those who overcome will dwell with Him where
there'll be no more tears

To the church in Laodicea, Jesus pointed out their
indifference and do-nothingness
And how allowing their wealth to make them callous and
content was hard to digest
Because of their lukewarm stance, they neglected making
Him their focus on earth
So Jesus warned He'd discipline them unless they repented,
yielding to His worth

God will accomplish His plan and in the end He will
conquer evil everywhere
For He is all-powerful, sovereign and majestic—none other
can ever compare
God sacrificed Christ the Lamb as the Savior for every
single sin of mankind
He alone is in control of the future, is worthy to designate
the days of end times

In the vision, Jesus showed John a revelation of Himself
using six symbolic seals
With creatures of nature as symbols of God's judgment,
mankind's sins revealed
The false Christ, war, famine, martyrs, terror, the
trumpets—signs of God's power
Will manifest themselves to all who have rejected God on
that day of the last hours

The seventh seal—the trumpets—will warn that judgment
is certain to all humanity
Will give unbelievers a chance to repent and herald the
Messiah's return decisively
The strong angel will descend to announce the final
judgment on each and everyone
Bringing the present world to an end with God prevailing,
Satan and unbelievers done

More visions appeared as clashing between God and Satan
unfolded for all its worth
And John caught sight of all sin, all atrocity and oppression
ever executed on earth
So clear was it until he saw the reason the battle between
good and evil transpired
And saw why Satan must be defeated, never again to do
evil, but forever retired

Evil will progressively rise with an antichrist as its ugly and
disastrous culmination
Then God's judgment will weigh in as the faithful and
unfaithful behold the separation
And the promise of eternity which true believers waited for
will then be realized
With persecution and suffering no more, they'll rejoice as
they inherit the prize

John's vision of the bowl judgments revealed the end at
hand—earth's very last dance
There would be no opportunity for unbelievers to repent, to
receive another chance
Then John reiterated the triumph of God, the marriage of
the Lamb and His bride
Which means the church, God's faithful believers, will
settle in forever by His side

Jesus as a warrior on a white horse was a vision of Him
subduing triumphantly
As He crossed the battle lines as conqueror and King and
emerged in victory
The final judgment will come to pass and Satan will meet
his just and final doom
And never again will he be a menace to anyone, for he'll
have no safety womb

After God's great judgment, He'll create a new eternal earth for
those who believe
For those whose names are written in the book of life, heaven will
be achieved
The new Jerusalem for Jews and Gentiles who've been faithful, no
matter the price
Will live on the new earth, joyful and peaceful in Paradise,
eternally with Christ

In conclusion, John's vision revealed the promise that
Christ will surely return
The tree of life awaits God's devoted followers to devour its
fruit faithfully earned
Because their sins were erased by Christ's death on the
cross and His resurrection
Partakers of that tree will live forevermore in that sweet city
of holy perfection

Just as Genesis commenced in Paradise, Revelation
concludes in a similar location
Sin destroyed the Garden of Eden, but the new Jerusalem
will be a perfect habitation
Amidst all the evil and affliction, Christ is summoning us
today to come and endure
To stand strong in the faith and be part of the
transformation—that's His signature

Read Revelation and examine yourself and your church—
strengths and deficiencies
Can your faith endure earth's struggles and pains or are
there shades of doubt or apathy?
Read Revelation and resist temptations that can trap you
and deceptively suck you in
Put your hope and faith in our Lord Christ Jesus and His
guarantee to return again

Read Revelation and accept the fact that God is the judge,
the only one in control
And no matter what occurs on this corrupt earth, only He
can make you whole
Read Revelation and accept God's assurance, the guarantee
of Christ's victory
Give your life to Him today and be assured of His promise,
of sweet eternity

Read Revelation and remove any obstacle hindering your
running the race to the end
Run with the saints Christ will return for, as eternity
beckons today—amen and amen!

Written on every page of the Bible
are wonders of God's grace and love.
On each of those pages we can discover
everything we need for life and
righteousness. May God awaken that
hunger inside for His Word and a will to
behold His goodness every day and live it.

Seek the LORD while He may be found.
Isaiah 55:6

Printed in the United States
35134LVS00005BA/1-42

9 781597 811767